TOYS WERE US

Platform Souls: the Trainspotter as Twentieth-century Hero
Blue Period: Notes from a Life in the Titillation Trade
Sweet Talk: The Secret History of Confectionery

TOYS WERE US

A HISTORY OF TWENTIETH-CENTURY TOYS
AND TOY-MAKING

NICHOLAS WHITTAKER

ORION

First published in Great Britain in 2001 by Orion
An imprint of Orion Books Ltd
Orion House, 5 Upper St Martin's Lane,
London WC2H 9EA

A CIP catalogue record for this book
is available from the British Library

ISBN 0 575 06808 6

Typeset in Great Britain by
Selwood Systems, Midsomer Norton

Printed and bound by
Butler & Tanner Ltd, Frome and London

INTRODUCTION

Our grandparents counted themselves lucky to get an orange in their Christmas stocking – so they tell us. Even today the fragrance of peel can make them come over all misty-eyed. Their reminiscences used to make us laugh – an orange and a sixpenny block of Cadbury's chocolate! But the wheel's come full circle. An orange is just what today's children want, too – an Orange pay-as-you-go mobile phone, with enough credit to last at least until Boxing Day. For the last Christmas of the twentieth century (officially, i.e., 25 December 2000) tens of thousands of British children demanded them. Orange is the new orange!

But I can already hear the protests. 'Mobile phones aren't toys,' some will say. *Au contraire.* In my book – and this *is* my book – I think we have to count them. Funny noises, twinkling lights, good to hold – mobile phones fulfil all the accepted criteria of a good toy. And the unofficial benchmarks, too: they confer status every bit as much as does possession of a Playstation 2, scooter or radio-controlled hot rod; they annoy grown-ups; and they're the cause of endless one-upmanship and brand rivalry.

In the past generation our concept of toys has had to expand. The Teddy bears and Lego sets are still there, still doing well, but a toy these days can be virtually anything that appeals to a child.

It goes some way towards explaining what happened to all those old-fashioned toyshops. Until the mid-seventies most towns had one. Or even two. Ours was called Toyland. To those old enough to qualify for this folk memory, such places were the Ali Baba's caves of childhood, overcrowded with exciting things, from the scooters and trikes in the window to the wooden drawers full of toy soldiers, each with its own label: 'WWII', 'Robin Hood', 'Roman & Trojan', 'Medieval'.

But the high street has changed and so has childhood. Children are just as likely to buy their 'toys' from computer shops, sports stores or oddly named places like the Car Phone Warehouse. Woolworth's still has some commitment to the traditional displays of toys – their Christmases are crazy, cute, crowded and colourful – but kids have the extra option of the Argos catalogue. Many will demand to be chauffeured to a dedicated out-of-town superstore like Toys R Us.

In days gone by kids wanted toy phones, toy typewriters and toy record-players, but now only the real thing will do. The dividing line between adult and child has become increasingly blurred. While children lobby for mobiles, palm-tops and smart hi-fis, their parents lurk around toy fairs and model shops looking for some memento of a fondly remembered childhood.

The paradox is that in other respects childhood seems to last longer. With the blurring of the divide, people are no longer sure when to start acting grown up or when to stop acting childishly. The time allowed for 'traditional' toys – Teddies, Matchbox cars, Lego – gets shorter and shorter. Left to their own devices children would probably be happy to stay in childhood for ever, but the Pied Pipers of the adult commercial world come calling for them at an ever earlier age. And off they must go into adulthood.

In many ways the word 'toys' is derogatory, patronising. No one likes to have their favourite possessions described so airily. And yet there is really little difference between the business-man's mobile and those touted by chattering pubescents the length and breadth of the country. Is a Dinky toy any less of a toy because it is collected by a nostalgic forty-year-old instead of noisy ten-year-old?

Yet, despite all these changes, it's remarkable how much things have remained the same. The 1913 edition of the cata-logue published by Gamages, the London department store, devoted 156 pages to toys: 25 pages of model trains, 9 of steam-powered toys, 20 for boats and aeroplanes (surely the cutting edge in 1913?), 6 full of toy soldiers, 12 of dolls, 5 of playsuits, and 3 each of chemistry sets and musical toys. Twenty pages were devoted to modelling and construction toys, while cutting-out, painting, beadwork, pokerwork and other craftwork toys took up a further seven pages.

Similar versions of most of these can still be found on the toys pages of the latest Argos catalogue, which must prove something about the enduring obsessions of childhood. Most would be familiar to children today and – were they given respite from the onslaught of TV commercials and peer pressure – would probably be just as absorbing. Mobiles and Playstations haven't ousted the old favourites; they've merely contributed to an ever-expanding choice.

As I ploughed through the old toy-trade journals, I tried to imagine those Christmases past, the cries of excitement as each present was unwrapped. We would recognise that much, certainly, but would we know what the hell they were on about?

'Wow – Nelsonics!'

Krom? Bamrang? Jerke? The Whip – 'the premier race game'. What on earth were these games and how did you play them? Can we imagine the excitement – or the arguments – that a Boxing Day game of Jerke or Bamrang would have triggered? Probably we can. I expect they'd be little different from the arguments that have erupted over Mousetrap or Scrabble for the past half-century.

None of us can guess whether the Playstation will still be around in 2102, or what awesome gadgets might have replaced it. But we do know that Meccano and the Teddy bear have been around for a hundred years already – and they'll probably still be around in 2102. Styles change, but substance is unchanging. It seems that children will always want some kind of humanoid shape to hold and direct, be it a doll, a toy soldier or a WWF wrestling figure. Their DNA is preprogrammed for construction kits, as it is for the musical toys that send their parents rushing for the paracetamol.

3

We all have – I hope – some Christmases of our own to treasure: hopelessly romanticised panes of frosted glass, a robin on a gatepost and carol singers with perfect pitch. Tosh, of course, but excusable tosh. Let no one pooh-pooh the real buzz that comes from opening presents: the wrapping paper, carefully folded and sellotaped, however beautiful, cast aside in seconds; those boxes that smell of plastic and new books and fresh rubber and cardboard. Sometimes there were so many boxes that you didn't know which one to go for first.

Everyone's memories are special. Unless you had one yourself, how can you understand my rapture at the Corgi Chipperfields' Circus Truck with its trailer, opening cage doors and plastic lion. No mere toy – it was as if a real circus had arrived in my living room with all the razzmatazz and animal roars. Or that huge metal lorry with its lovely thick tyres and its load of two cable drums – real wood – that you could let down from the back. Not forgetting all those little games – solitaire, exquisite dominoes, my first chess set – and a square plastic maze with its shivering blob of mercury that you had to guide to the centre. It demanded a steady hand and unusual reserves of patience for a nine-year-old: one tremor and it split itself in two or four, scattering its silver blobettes in all directions.

We've all had our favourites. Some hold on to their old Teddy bears and dolls for the rest of their lives. Many of us carry an aching nostalgia for the ones that get lost or are purposelessly destroyed in juvenile attempts at 'cool', only for their destruction to be deeply regretted later.

Our children, lucky beggars, are not yet burdened by nostalgia. We grown-ups remember our Dinky cars and dolls with exaggerated sentiment, but will today's kids one day get misty-eyed about the Christmas Day when they unwrapped their Playstation, Game Boy or new mobile? I think so. They will still get the whiff of that elusive fragrance of newness that will always excite, no matter what the toy itself might be. Maybe they'll even remember their very first text message, pressed out with eager fingers as the snowflakes fell outside and the aroma of roasting turkey wafted in from the kitchen.

We would (and do!) pay large sums to get our toys back. Old toys are big business. No longer allowed to moulder in attics, they have status. Collectable, serious, the province of bow-tied antique dealers, old dolls, Dinky cars and Hornby-Dublo trains have been elevated to the status of antiques. Kids are even advised to stow their Buzz Lightyear figures and their Sylvanian Family sets with the hint that they might – just might – become the sought-after antiques of the 2050s.

So I start from the premise of nostalgia. Childhood is and should be a time of fantasy, of play and discovery, of – that much maligned word – innocence. I tried not to make too many wisecracks. Admittedly it's hard to resist sometimes. How many adults can help their bemusement on coming face to face with My Little Pony? Who can gaze on its poseable head, on a face of superlative cuteness, its jewelled eyes a-twinkling and not feel a streak of cruel amusement? It's easy enough to mock My Little Pony – and the girls who adore them so. Likewise, the little lads who think that WWF wrestling figures are the bee's knees. Easy, yes, but pure hypocrisy, especially from a man who still hankers after a model-railway layout for his loft, complete with electrically operated signals and miniature porters lugging even more miniature suitcases.

Eschewing any hard and fast methodology, I decided to include whatever I came across, including mobile phones. The hawk-eyed will doubtless point out the dozens of favourite toys that have been omitted and a token apology would be apt here. But there was no way I could include everything and it would have been foolish to attempt some kind of definitive survey of the twentieth century's toys. Despite my best efforts, some toys held on to their secrets. It's possible that the hula hoop has been implicated in a fatal accident somewhere in the world, but if it has, I didn't hear about it.

At the end of the day, of course, toys are just products. Forget the fairy-tales – no toy-maker ever had white hair and pince-nez, no toy-maker did it purely for love. Money is always the bottom line. Profits. Shareholders to please. Targeted marketing. Toys never had that much meaning to the folk who made them. They were just by-products of the plastics industry or someone's obsession with inventing. Children are the only ones who know the true value of toys.

1900-1920

Children are easily bored. That's always been the bottom line – a harsh truth for Victorian parents as much as it is for those of the twenty-first century. When a devoted dad spends hours – days even – building a working crane for his kids a yawn is all it takes to make the whole exercise seem a complete waste of time.

And so it must have seemed to Frank Hornby, a shipping clerk in late Victorian Liverpool, who loved making simple mechanical toys for his young sons. Their fascination was real enough – but only ever temporary. The next day they always wanted a new toy. An age-old dilemma it appears...

Then Frank had one of those 'Eureka!' moments. Why not construct his toys with interchangeable and reusable parts, strips that could be fixed together to make one model, and then, when the children found it impossibly passé, Dad could simply unbolt the whole lot and reassemble the strips to form another toy? Yesterday's crane could become today's car and tomorrow's boat.

Hornby set to work, cutting and perforating his strips of copper, with preset lengths and hole-spacings that remain the same a century later.

'Mechanics Made Easy', as Hornby dubbed his system, was granted a patent in 1901. Local toyshops, around which he trudged with samples, greeted his idea with scepticism. A tin box full of nuts and bolts and metal strips and rods? It didn't look like the kind of idea that would go down too well with children. Even junior Victorians could have sophisticated expectations of their playthings. But driven by an evangelical belief in the new toy, Hornby persisted and shopkeepers eventually agreed to take a few of the boxes.

They sold like the proverbial hot cakes. Or even hot rods. Mechanics Made Easy was acclaimed as 'real engineering in miniature' – a true enough claim and an educational benefit repeatedly stressed in the product's publicity. By 1910, after a name change to the more snappy Meccano, Hornby's system was well established and toyshops were able to offer a range of seven kits. Starting at a modest three shillings and sixpence, sets went up to a princely six guineas – a month's wages for many working-class folk. Components became more sophisticated too, with angle girders and polished brass wheels in addition to the nickel-plated strips. The guiding principle behind Meccano was that a boy would progress from one set to the next by purchasing 'accessory outfits'. Thus, a boy who started with Set No. 3 could then buy Set No. 3A – which converted his set into a No. 4. And so on. It is a system that has remained unchanged throughout Meccano's hundred-year history.

Though first and foremost a businessman, Frank Hornby held firm beliefs about the best ways to develop a boy's mind and mechanical abilities. This evangelism was advanced by the arrival in 1916 of *Meccano Magazine* – 'to help Meccano Boys have more fun than other boys'. And why wouldn't they? Meccano now offered even more new parts, including braced girders, spoked wheels, and sprocket chains and wheels. With these components on hand, boys were encouraged to tackle a range of ambitious projects. The Meccano weaving loom, for example, was an amazing array of pulleys, sprocket wheels and gears which wove cloth. The Meccano Eiffel Tower – though majestic size-wise – seemed sadly static by comparison and looked like a simple job.

In addition to the construction suggestions included with each Meccano set, Hornby wanted boys to tackle projects of their own. Meccano competitions – graded by age to give the youngest boys a chance – were regular events up and down the country and prizewinners often had the honour of seeing their creations adopted as officially approved projects in future manuals. *Meccano Magazine* also carried a suggestions page, edited by the delightfully named Spanner, a pseudonym adopted by a succession of staff writers. Small prizes were awarded for the best ideas, which were published in the magazine. Readers were also asked to suggest new parts for the system. One of the most frequent requests was for flexible metal plates: Meccano's perforated strips may have provided sound evidence of engineering principles in practice, but the finished constructions were sadly lacking in realism. When they were introduced, flexible plates did much to flesh out the skeletal look which many of the models had and gave them a more true-to-life appearance.

While 'strip down and rebuild' universality was one of Meccano's main selling points, some of the constructions were so magnificent that many boys wanted to keep and show off the models they'd made. Those who chose to display rather than dismantle could find plenty of accessories with which to customise their creations. For the Meccano cruise liner, for instance, toyshops could offer an astonishing array of funnels, all decked out in the colours of P&O, Blue Star, Cunard, Ellerman, Holland-Afrika – or any of twenty-three other Merchant Navy liveries.

The Meccano Boy – 'so happy, so infectious that all boys love me and smile with sheer joy when they see me' – had become an icon of childhood and his praises were sung by a succession of copywriters. Though rival manufacturers were not blessed by such an instantly recognisable figurehead, British toyshops offered children plenty of other construction sets. Among the most well known were Pintung, Metallo-Tringon, Anchor Blocks, Erektit, Kliptiko and Structator. Stripwork promised 'an endless variety of models' from its simple strips of wood. Wenebrik, described as an 'all-British architectural toy', consisted of small tinplate pieces in sets – bricks, slates, ridge tiles, gutters, chimneys and so on – and resulted in finished models which were firm and rigid. Perhaps the most natural looking of all the options were Lotts bricks, miniature building-blocks which were made of artificial stone.

There was a similar passion for constructional toys in the USA. In 1913 former Olympic pole-vaulter (Gold Medal,

1908) A.C. Gilbert invented the Erector Set, a motorised toy consisting of steel components with which children could build models of everything from Ferris wheels and skyscrapers to gramophones and microscopes. Inspired by watching younger children poking sticks and pencils in thread bobbins, Charles Pajeau developed Tinker Toys, based on the same principles as the Erector Set, but aimed at younger children. In 1916 John Lloyd Wright, son of the famous architect Frank, invented Lincoln Logs, interlocking toy logs with which children could build a variety of imaginative structures. Wright was supposedly inspired by his father's designs of the earthquake-proof Imperial Hotel in Tokyo, presumably not built of logs but put together along broadly similar lines.

With so many constructional toys around, Meccano's lawyers were constantly on the lookout for rivals and copy-cats and it wasn't long before court injunctions were taken out against any that too closely resembled Meccano: the American Model Builder, for instance. The outcome of this spat is unclear, but if Meccano was based on simple and *universal* engineering principles, as Hornby claimed, then it would be hard for his company to prove any infringement.

There were many other toys that aimed to cash in on the creative bent of young men. Clockmaking Made Easy – 'will appeal to boys very strongly' – was just one of many practical gifts a boy might receive from doting parents. Perhaps it was a trifle over-optimistic, but much was made of boyish ingenuity and resourcefulness – attributes rarely encouraged in girls. Nor were their talents limited to things mechanical: 'Boys of taste and intelligence can do anything with this material,' claimed the firm behind Novissima, a new creative material which was basically just dyed sawdust. The epitome of 'waste not want not', it was a fiendishly simple but lucrative use for all those tons of sawdust produced in the making of thousands of wooden toys. 'Anything' might have been poetic licence, but Novissima was certainly ideal as a basic material for making naturalistic backdrops for Meccano constructions and early model-railway layouts.

Although Hornby was making his mark and the loyally named William Britain was already well established, Germany reigned supreme as a major supplier to the toyshops of the United Kingdom in the decades before the First World War. When it came to clockwork trains and mechanical men, few could beat the tinsmiths of Berlin and Leipzig. Established firms like Lehmann produced many lovable toys in tinplate – a clockwork horse and cart set and a 'motor cyclist with lady passenger'. The Erratic Motorist was fitted with an eccentric cog to interrupt any linear progress. But it was Gustav the Busy Miller who really flew the flag for Teutonic tinsmithery. Aided by clockwork, Gustav climbed a ladder to the top of his windmill and came back down with a sack of flour on his head – all while the sails kept rotating.

The lead Zeppelin has only ever been a figure of speech, but the clever toy-makers who worked at the Marklin factory did bring out a tin balloon based on the original Zeppelin design. There was also Lehmann's clockwork toy Zeppelin, fitted with an oversized propeller so that when suspended from the ceiling it could 'fly' – albeit in small circles.

Undoubted wizards as they were at clockwork and fashioning strips of tin into toys, maybe busy millers and haughty airships smacked too much of hard work and one-upmanship. Tin was ideal for funnier things, especially as it was magnetic. In America they'd come up with Old Daddy Tin Whiskers. This head of a bald, clean-shaven man was stamped in relief and painted in natural colours. 'It can be closely examined and will seem utterly impossible for hair to grow on it. Yet by the aid of a Magic Ring – to the casual observer just an ordinary finger ring – you can produce a luxuriant crop of hair on its head, as well as eyebrows, moustache and beard. You can *see* it grow!' Old Daddy's hair was iron grey – which was only to be expected as it was made of iron filings.

In 1900 there were six different gauges for toy railways, ranging from the comparatively small 0 (1¼ inches to the foot) to the massive gauge 4 (2¾₁₆ inches to the foot). Model railway scales were fixed by the individual whims of the manufacturers.

11

Appearance was the main thing. Even manufacturers who used the same gauge spoiled the chances of interconnectivity by using a range of wheel sizes and couplings. Building an integrated scale-model railway was impossible.

At the 1891 Leipzig Toy Fair Marklin had introduced trains and track parts with geometric curves, straights, points and crossings in five different scales. Founded in 1859, Marklin had the distinction of being the leading manufacturer of toy trains in the world, and so their new standards were bound to be followed by others.

- No.5 gauge (120mm or 4⅝ inches to 1 foot)
- No.4 gauge (75mm or 3 inches to 1 foot)
- No.3 gauge (67mm or 2⅝ inches to 1 foot)
- No.2 gauge (54mm or 2⅛ inches to 1 foot)
- No.1 gauge (48mm or 1⅞ inches to 1 foot)

In 1900 came the new 0 gauge of 35mm or 1⅜ inches to the foot; this allowed train sets to be set up in smaller homes.

In 1912 a US manufacturer began production of a range of trains based on Marklin's No.2 gauge. However, they assumed that the measurements in Marklin's literature were taken *between* the rails, normal practice in the USA. But the Europeans measured *from the middle* of each rail. Other manufacturers who took up the standards renamed them – and so their 75mm gauge was known as No.3 and their 67mm gauge as No.2. By comparison, the Tower of Babel must have seemed like a model of clarity.

Larger gauges soon fell out of favour, with nothing larger than No.1 appearing after the First World War, and even this had faded by the 1930s. 0 gauge became popular as the price and size made railways accessible to the middle classes and it was soon miniaturised when Marklin introduced their 00 gauge of about ⅞ inches (22mm). Bing of Nurnberg bettered this with a 'tabletop' range in 1921, which was ⅝ inches (between the rails), chosen because it was half 0 gauge. This was taken up by Henry Greenly for the British market in 1923.

But German dominance was about to be challenged.

In 1901, aged just twenty-two, a young New Yorker by the name of Lionel Cowen created a battery-powered train engine. Far from being intended as a child's toy, it was originally conceived to be nothing more than a clever window display, a 'mobile advertisement' for products in a Manhattan store. To everyone's surprise, customers proved more interested in purchasing the toy train than the merchandise inside the shop.

From such inauspicious beginnings arose Lionel Trains.

As a child, Cowen already had a mechanical mind. Intrigued by the rolling eyes in one of his sister's dolls, he cracked open its head to see how they worked. He claimed to have invented the electric doorbell while at school, and it might have been taken further had not his teacher discouraged him by remarking that nothing could beat a good old-fashioned rap with the knuckles. After dropping out of New York College and Columbia University, Cowen became an apprentice to a manufacturer of dry-cell batteries. Eventually he landed a job at the Acme Lamp Company and by 1899 the 20-year-old had already filed his first patent. It was for a device that could safely ignite a photographic flash without endangering the photographer's whiskers. Following this Cowen won a US Navy contract to equip 24,000 mines with foolproof detonators. The story goes that the mines were delivered to his apartment in New York and he worked until the small hours every night fitting his devices. Little did his neighbours know that they were sitting on enough high explosive to blow away half of Manhattan.

In 1900 Cowen and a colleague from Acme founded the Lionel Manufacturing Company. His first idea, dreamed up during a hot spell while waiting for a cool breeze, was an electric fan. It was a simple concept and easy to construct. After quickly assembling a few examples he set about marketing the product. Things looked promising – until the weather turned cool and no one wanted to know.

It was shortly after this, while walking through Manhattan, that Cowen stopped at a shop window to look at a push-along train which was being used as a promotional gimmick. How much more effective, he thought, if the train were moving under its own steam – just like a real train. And it couldn't be easier: fit the train with an electric motor and lay down track in a continuous circle. Such a display could go on indefinitely without needing any attention.

His first model-train customer was Ingersoll, the owner of the shop where Cowen had seen the push train. His first commercially available Lionel 'train set' – the 'Electric Express' – was simply a large open gondola propelled by a fan motor. The track was formed by two parallel steel strips inserted into slotted tiles.

In 1902 the first Lionel Trains catalogue was published, with containers of acid and lead plates which converted household current for train use and dry-cell batteries for homes without electricity. In 1903 they brought out a more sophisticated set, with an electric B & O locomotive and motorised derrick car. In 1906 Cowen added a third rail to carry the current and standardised the outer rails at $2\frac{1}{8}$ inches apart. This was the system adopted by most other manufacturers. Their first pre-assembled train sets were sold with a choice of two steam engines, two passenger cars, seven freight cars and a transformer. In 1915, to compete with the growing number of manufacturers offering train sets, Cowen started production of railway sets in 0 gauge, which was proving to be the most popular standard size in Europe and the USA.

Over in Britain the frontrunner in the world of model railways was the Northampton firm founded by the gloriously named Wenman J. Bassett-Lowke. After meeting up with established toy-makers Ignaz and Stefan Bing at the 1900 Paris Exhibition he started a long association with German toy companies. Though they already exported many toys to the UK, Bassett-Lowke encouraged the Germans to perfect their scale models and develop smaller toys, Anglicised to Bassett-Lowke's specifications. The first Bing product for Bassett-Lowke was the $2\frac{1}{2}$-inch-gauge LNWR *Black Prince*, the first Continental model to be based on a British prototype. Building on the popularity of this locomotive, Bassett-Lowke was able to suggest all manner of uniquely British ideas that the Germans might otherwise not have conceived. Bing's Victoria Station, for instance, another Bassett-Lowke idea, proved to be a great hit and was a star feature of the 1906 Gamages' catalogue. Colourfully lithographed and designed to be illuminated from inside by candles, the miniature station sported numerous architectural details, including a WH Smith and Sons bookstall.

Before long, Bassett-Lowke, widely regarded as one of the founding fathers of model railways, was producing his own designs. Much more faithful in scale and detail than anything previously, such attention to detail did much to popularise model railways in general and those of Bassett-Lowke in particular.

Much effort was put into improving toy railways, even though some traditionalists insisted on the continued use of wood. Simpull sets made use of wooden track for their toy locomotives and carriages – 'better than flimsy wobbly tin-plate'. Joiboy wooden trains were advertised as 'practically unbreakable. So sturdy that a fifteen stone man can stand on a single truck without breaking it!' As if any dignified gent would want to do such a thing! The smaller trains were about three feet in length, but the largest – there was one eight feet long – was commodious enough for several children.

Electricity posed an ever-present danger. People were remarkably blasé and ham-fisted, nothing like the wiring-literate toy consumers of the twenty-first century. Some of the first electric train sets had to be plugged directly into the mains – with blindingly obvious dangers – but even the advent of trans-formers didn't make model railways entirely safe. Users were issued with dire warnings to treat their transformers with care. Sound advice it was, too: fix the wires to the wrong terminals and – *fizz! crackle! scorch!* – instead of 110 volts being reduced to a harmless 3, it could be stepped up to a lethal 1,140!

A toy with much less potential for homicide is the Teddy bear, which in the long-winded psychobabble of one modern American 'represents a study in endurance of basic values in a century wrought with change and advanced technology'. A valid enough viewpoint, but one that might equally apply to Cabbage Patch Kids or My Little Pony. Even caring for a bleeping Tamagotchi can call for as much devotion – if not more – than the soft option of looking after a silent and patient stuffed animal.

Teddy bear fans – and there are collectors worldwide – attribute all kinds of values to *their* toy. They enthuse with a spiritual elitism that ultimately jars. They've even invented a name for themselves – arctophiles – friends of the bear. It's a sure sign that something is awry in what should be a simple relationship between humans and their toys. Everyone knows a Teddy bear is cuddly, lovable, cute and loyal, but why do arctophiles feel a need to voice that sentiment so loudly, in so many books, in such squeamishly fulsome prose? From Archibald Ormsby-Gore, Sir John Betjeman's bear, to Sebastian Flyte's Aloysius, Teddy bears are stars. From Pooh to Paddington to Pudsey Teddy bears proliferate. For a while the bears had some serious rivals, such as Billy Possum –

an American invention aimed at usurping Ted's supremacy – and Bob Bunty, a British bunny rabbit whose proclaimed mission 'is to supplant the Teddy bear', but Ted has seen off all-comers, and who would begrudge him his place at the top? That Teddy bears feel good is undisputed and only a curmudgeon would want to mock the pleasure they've given to millions. What grates is the heavy-handed 'aren't we all softies really?' feel to it all.

Stuffed bears had been around for many years before anyone thought of calling them Teddies. Before that they were known simply as

Early naval teddy bear. 'What grates is the heavy-handed: "aren't we all softies really?"' (V&A)

16

bears or bruins, no more privileged in nursery mythology than the scores of other soft toys such as the Terryer Toys Company's dogs – Friskie and Ruffus or cats – Fluffie and Lappit – all with patented movable eyes to make them extra charming.

Bears acquired their new name courtesy of US President Theodore Roosevelt. The story goes that in the autumn of 1902 he was on a hunting trip in Mississippi, staying as a guest of certain parties who were lobbying to have a new state line drawn up with neighbouring Louisiana. Knowing his fondness for backwoods sport, his hosts arranged a bear hunt for him. Unfortunately, no bears volunteered themselves for death by shotgun – even one wielded by a US President. Embarrassed, his hosts found a bear cub and cynically shooed the poor creature towards where Roosevelt was standing. Sportingly, Theodore refused to slaughter a sitting target. Perhaps it was superstition. After all, Roosevelt only got the President's job because his predecessor had been shot dead by an anarchist.

Stories about this principled stand quickly went around, although it took some time before the bear cub was cemented in the story. One early version claimed the unwitting target was an old and lame 230-pound beast that the President refused to use for sport; he did, however, encourage one of his hosts to dispatch it out of 'kindness'. A topical cartoon appeared in the *Washington Post* and everyone told each other what a fine and honourable gentleman Mr Roosevelt was. To cash in on the public's 'aah!' response to the event, toy-makers thought it would be a good time to give their stuffed bears a marketing push. Shortly afterwards another newspaper cartoonist created two bears – Teddy B and Teddy G – otherwise known as 'the Roosevelt Bears'. Their adventures became the subject of a popular weekly strip and in May 1906 the American toy-trade magazine *Playthings* carried an advert for soft toys based on Teddy B and Teddy G, now dubbed simply Teddy's bears (note the apostrophe). By October the possessive element appears to have been dropped from adverts: whether this was deliberate or just the result of sloppy grammar by a copywriter is unclear, but by that time the toys had become simply and universally known as Teddy bears.

Over in Britain the Roosevelt story was challenged by a rival faction who claimed that Edward VII (just as much of a Ted as the President, of course) had a fondness for the koala 'bears' newly arrived at London Zoo, and that the name came from this.

On both sides of the Atlantic aeroplanes were all the rage, and a firm with the somewhat basic name of New Things Ltd offered children a wide choice of play aircraft – the Prince Bi-Plane, Regent Monoplane, Dragon-Fly and a Royal Monoplane. 'All are actual flyers,' they promised. The Aeolus Airship – described as exactly similar to a Zeppelin – came 'complete with all the necessary apparatus for producing the gas for inflation'. And lest the mention of gas unnerved any parents, the adverts hastened to add that 'there is not the slightest chance of an explosion'. By calculated use of ballast the Aeolus could be made to remain at any desired height and, depending on the angle of its rudder, would travel in a line or in circles. 'A source of endless amusement,' claimed the advertisements, relaying what was destined to become one of the most overused phrases in the history of toy-making.

With the First World War looming, the potential for airborne belligerence had already been recognised – and nothing sold quite as well as war toys. As well as toy aeroplanes – which were only approximate representations of contemporary aircraft – one of the bestsellers in the shops was the Finbat model war-kite. War-kites were more or less an early version of the hang-glider and were being used in Europe to lift military observers high enough into the sky for them to report back on enemy territory. There's a philosophical point here: which was the prototype and which was the copycat? Were Finbats based on real-life 'spy in the sky' adventuring or was the military idea just a large-scale manned version of children's kites?

The uses of bears and kites are fairly obvious but the shelves of Edwardian toyshops were also home to dozens of board games whose purpose we can only guess at now. The names are intriguing enough, but what the assembled players argued over remains a mystery. Shooting the Chute; Climbing St Bruno; Tildof; Fairyland; John Bull Puzzle; Scrimmo; Great Raid; Bombardo Pool; Jiggeries; Bogey; Twirlette; Madrolo; Kibosh – 'the game of winking skulls'.

Originally known as Moksha-Patamu, Snakes and Ladders had its origins in a Hindu game used to teach children about the religion. The base square for each ladder – a 'good' square – allowed a player to ascend to a higher life, whereas the squares hosting the snakes' mouths – the 'bad' squares – represented the numerous forms of evil. 'Good' squares on the traditional prototype included such as Faith, Reliability, Generosity, Knowledge and Asceticism; while the far more numerous 'evil' squares featured Disobedience, Vanity, Vulgarity, Theft, Lying, Drunkenness, Debt, Rage, Greed, Pride, Murder and (usually on square 99 to trap anyone who was starting to feel smug) Lust. Number 100, if one ever attained it after all these trials, presumably represented Nirvana.

Introduced to Britain by returning old hands from India, the game's moral dimension appealed to the Victorians, leading to considerable success when it was first produced for the home market in 1892. Renamed Snakes and Ladders, the game was pretty much the same as the Hindu original, though the vices and virtues were renamed to fit in with prevailing Victorian ideals. Landing on squares such as Penitence, Thrift and Industry, for instance, elevated a player up a ladder to squares labelled Grace, Fulfilment and Success. Similarly, anyone unlucky enough to land on Indolence, Indulgence or Disobedience was doomed to slither down the snake towards Poverty, Illness and Disgrace.

Though still popular in the West, Snakes and Ladders has long discarded the moral purposes it was designed for. Some versions even have a suspiciously PC slant, with far more numerous ladders than snakes, just to make sure little Johnny doesn't get too upset with the vicissitudes of fate.

One board game which has not proved to be quite so enduring was Find Alf Smith. It was something of a craze at Christmas

1913 and was supposedly based on a real-life event. During the general election of 1910 newspapers had reported the story of poor old Mr Smith, a working-class Nottingham man whose family was on the brink of starvation. The press was eager to get his opinions on the new government, but Alf and his kin had apparently moved on to Leicester. Enquiries by intrepid reporters failed to find him there as he'd moved on to Bermondsey in London. Weary reporters, on arriving there, weren't too surprised to be informed that he'd gone to live in Walthamstow. Of course, despite an exhausting survey and detective work in every labour exchange and pub in north London, he couldn't be found there either. The box lid issued the challenge: 'The arduous task now devolves to you − find Alf Smith!'

Another politics-based board game was *Wait and See*, in which players had to second-guess the identity of the next prime minister. Would-be political pundits might just as well have turned to Triplicity − a fortune-telling card game. 'Mirth! Mystery! Magic!' it promised on the pack, but it did insist that players 'can tell fortunes as well as any astronomer or gypsy'. Just as reliable as opinion polls then ...

The following year the First World War made its mark. Trade magazines foamed with stern admonishments and out-right contempt for those who put profit before patriotism: 'Buy English goods or goods made by our allies' was one appeal. 'Be patriotic and trade with your countrymen.'

Despite a grudging professional admiration for the work-manship of European toy-makers, people now had a good reason to scorn foreign toys. Rivals dissected any imports with the ruthlessness of a pathologist doing an autopsy. Dolls imported from France were found to be fitted with heads made in Saxony and bodies manufactured in the workshops of Nuremberg. Only the clothes could claim to have any truly French origins. To resentful doll-makers in Britain the inevitable result of this commercial crossbreeding could only be 'a heavy German Gretchen with stolid limbs and ox-eyed demeanour'.

'Cut all Hun connection from now on!' roared the toy-trade press, warning toyshop owners that 'the wily Hun are continuing to trade via Holland, Sweden and Switzerland', and to be especially careful to check the provenance of any new stock on their shelves. This boycott certainly had some effect on German manufacturers and many were forced to offload their output cheaply on to the home market. This resulted in some bizarre spectacles – such as German children blithely playing with train sets called *Northern Express* and battleships named *Lord Nelson*, toys that had originally been made in Germany for the British market.

Even before the war British-style names had been useful in selling an idea of quality, like Windsor Building Bricks – 'better than the German,' boasted the adverts.

The Germans were so much to the fore of public consciousness that one wonders what the toy industry would have done without them. Though no longer welcome as toy-makers they at least provided a focus for all manner of toys and games. Besides being the sworn enemies of every boy acting out the war with his cap gun, the enemy popped up in all kinds of board games, from one called Recruiting for Kitchener's Army to another with the more prosaic title of Shooting the Germans. Big Co Games introduced Dash to Berlin, in which the object was for players representing France, Russia, Britain and Belgium to be first to occupy Berlin. Also based on the war were Blockade, Aeroplanes and Zeppelins, and Silver Bullet, a game which consisted of a maze leading to Berlin with a steel ball which disappeared and returned to its starting-point. More direct was Pills for Kaiser Bill, in which the object was to make the average British child's enemy number one 'swallow your red, white and blue pills', which players presumably hoped were laced with some noxious substance. The Noisy Billet was a comical shooting game which featured five numbered Tommies and a spring-loaded pistol with which to shoot the rowdy recruits and so enforce silence. Standing out among the hundreds of games and toys coloured by the ongoing war was a board game dubbed Peace with Honour. Described as 'a highly interesting game', the object was not to obliterate the beastly Germans but to come to a sensible détente.

Toy guns, of one kind or another, were always in demand. Models ranged from the mischievous Warspite Pea Repeater to ruggedly named armaments like the Scout, the Drake, the Celt or the Revenge, toy revolvers which used explosive caps for added realism. There were double-barrelled versions such as the Zulu and Ajax, the Spitfire cork pistol and a fearsome repeating pea pistol capable of firing twenty shots in rapid succession. The Little Dandy topped them all: a pea pistol and pop gun in one.

Liquid pistols were another favourite. Water was the obvious ammunition, but more mischievous spirits would often opt for ink or sour milk (or worse!). Even so, it's hard to believe the claims for the Repeating Liquid Pistol: 'will stop the most vicious dog (or man) without permanent injury'. The target might not be permanently injured, but you've got to think that the owner of the pistol might be, once they've dispensed a soaking. Another aptly named example was the Sokum Water Pistol. As for the Viking, it seems highly unlikely that the horned invaders would have been able to rape and pillage their way through England with such a wet idea in weaponry!

'Boys will be boys' was the usual excuse, but such antics were not always looked on so indulgently. Three youths in one Bristol court case were fined twenty shillings each for terrorising passers-by with pop guns. And one pellet-firing toy gun – fully cocked and loaded – fired at such velocity that it was responsible for the death of one Private Yeo of the Royal Hussars. In May 1909, in a court case in Sheffield brought under the Pistols Act, the prosecution's demonstration with a toy pistol led to one of the JPs suffering a bloodied ear. This incident understandably coloured the argument and persuaded the bench that toy pistols were indeed dangerous and that the two youths brought up before them should be convicted of possessing offensive weapons.

During the First World War toy guns were viewed with even more suspicion. Under the Defence of the Realm Act, toy traders who wished to sell them were required to obtain a permit from the military authorities of the district. Offenders risked a five-pound fine.

All in all, toy bows and arrows seemed a far safer idea, especially now that some toy-maker had come up with the bright idea of fitting the missiles with 'vacuum tips' – in other words the rubber suckers that are still around today. There were also toy 'big guns', including a naval twelve-pounder, trench bomb-thrower, ack-ack gun and a French 75mm. Model tanks with caterpillar tracks were also proving to be big sellers in the toyshops – even with a massive two-guinea price tag. Model entrenchments could be bought, complete with a complement of twelve tin soldiers. With such war toys still proving popular, it seems that the true mud and blood horrors of trench warfare had yet to come across to a section of the population. There was even a minor craze for Conchy dolls. Patriots looked aghast at the idea of toys being used for such blatant politicising: 'One looks like a red-hot socialist,' complained a trade editorial. 'Another is a whiskered villain, the third surely a resident of Colney Hatch. Let the doll-making trade be a cut above these characters. There are surely much more pleasant subjects.'

Yes, like safety perhaps. In the absence of stringent regulations, anyone could set themselves up as a doll-maker. Accidents – and even fatalities – were common. The two-year-old son of Alfred Septimus Hunter, a Hull shipwright, died horribly after he fell over while scampering around the house with his doll. Normally it would have resulted in nothing more than a bruise and a few tears. But the doll's head broke off, exposing a metal spike which pierced the little lad's mouth. His mother rushed him off to hospital, carrying him in her arms for over a mile, but the poor mite was bleeding so much that he died before help could be reached.

Jigsaw puzzles – or dissected puzzles as they were known – were less dangerous (choking aside). Introduced at the turn of the century, they really began to catch on as the privations of the war restricted many of society's former pleasures. Those who scorned such novelties were reminded that they offered a 'new industry as well as a new amusement'. The puzzles were described as 'much in vogue' and this was meant literally – in vogue – not just a cheap craze for the hoi polloi. Tuck's Zag-Zaw Puzzles, according to their advertisement, were

> the preferred amusement of royalty, society and the great public. The curtailment of social pleasures during the war leaves the leisured classes more time than formerly for intellectual recreation... and this the successful building up of a Zag-Zaw Picture Puzzle undoubtedly supplies.

Jigsaw puzzles also proved an ideal medium for a message, but it is doubtful if any of the establishment figures included in the above would have been inclined to purchase the heroic Mrs Pankhurst tableau issued by the Suffragette Puzzle Company.

Protecting domestic trade was a neverending problem. No sooner had Germany been marginalised than the warning cry had to be changed to 'Look out for Japan!' Toy-makers there – predictably dubbed 'wily Orientals' – had seen a lucrative gap in the market now that the British had no wish to trade with their enemies.

In Japan itself there were plenty of games unknown in the West but seemingly ripe for export. One example was *menko*, a game dating back to the 1700s. Players threw circular or rectangular playing cards on to the ground. The aim was to flip over an opponent's card by throwing your card on top of it. Popular mostly with boys, the cards were decorated with pictures of comic-book heroes, baseball players, film stars and other celebrities. This old-fashioned game produced echoes – and generated far more publicity and money – when it was reinvented in the Western world as POGS in the 1990s.

Perhaps the most traditional toy was the kite, or *tako*. They were made in a variety of shapes – square, triangular and hexagonal – but strong vibrant colours were as important as shape and the kites were decorated with traditional pictures, patterns and calligraphy. One notable kind was the *yakkodako*, designed to resemble human figures in comical poses. Wealthier families had *yakkodako* kites made in the likenesses of their servants. Communities often pooled their efforts to build and launch enormous kites, up to a hundred square metres in size. Kite wars, in which players tried to sever their opponents' kite strings, were also popular.

Japanese girls had more genteel pursuits. *Hanetsuki*, a game dating back hundreds of years, was similar to badminton but without a net. The shuttlecock was made from a large seed with feathers attached, and the bats fashioned from a rectangular piece of wood, often decorated with traditional images – girls in kimonos, Kabuki actors and so on. While Japanese children still play *hanetsuki* today, there is also a big market in collecting the bats for their decorative and nostalgia value.

Japanese children also enjoy playing cards known as *karuta*, which are a similar size and shape to Western playing cards, but with pictures, words and poems on them. In one popular version of the game – *iroha karuta* – one player is designated as the 'reader' and holds one set of cards with proverbs and sayings on them; the other players gather around a spread of cards with the first letter or word of the saying and a picture on them. When the reader starts to quote a saying from one of his cards, the players try to find the matching card from the array in front of them. Whoever finds the card first wins the round and keeps the card. The player who collects most cards wins.

While these Japanese children learned their proverbs through play, back in Britain, as pinafored girls played with their skipping-ropes, ragamuffin boys in short trousers would gather in corners to play with their Brilliant Pretty Dicks. 'Look at the little fulkers,' the headmaster might say to his colleagues. They were not being unduly cynical about the rewards of teaching: fulking was the most common method of shooting marbles along the ground; the marble is balanced in the crooked forefinger and the thumb flicked on to the ball with whatever force is required. This method was less accurate than 'knuckling down', the modus operandi favoured by experts, but it was probably more fun! The Brilliant Pretty Dicks, as you've probably guessed, were among the marbles that were fulked. But these were no ordinary fulkers' balls: highly polished, they enjoyed an exchange rate of one to four of the ordinary, unglazed marbles that were the common currency of the game.

Marbles have a long history and can be traced back 3,000 years. Examples made from round stones, nuts or pottery have been found in Egyptian pyramids and in Native American burial mounds. Roman literature had many references to marbles and it is probable that the Romans took the game to all parts of their empire. In Britain an annual Good Friday marble tournament has been played in Tinsley Green for the past 300 years. Isaiah Thomas's *Pretty Little Pocket Book* of 1787 has a verse about playing marbles while in *Songs of Innocence* William Blake illustrated his poem 'The Schoolboy' with a picture of three boys playing marbles, one of the earliest known depictions of the game.

Marbles were usually fashioned from common stone, though some were made from real marble. China and pottery marbles were introduced around 1800. The *Boys' Own Book* of 1829 contained a page giving ratings for all the different varieties: cheapest were Dutch glazed clay or yellow stone with black or brown spots; top of the range were those of pink stone with red veins. Glass marbles had been made in Venice from the beginning of the nineteenth century, but it wasn't until 1846, when a German glassblower invented 'marble scissors' that production became easy enough to make them commercially viable. Nevertheless, the majority of marbles were still made of the cheaper clay for several years. Glass marbles first started appearing widely around 1860, with the brighter swirl type produced in England only early in the twentieth century.

Simple machines for making glass marbles were first introduced in America in the 1890s, and in 1905 Martin Christensen of Akron, Ohio, designed a machine capable of producing perfectly round specimens. Glass is melted in a furnace and poured out, with coloured glass injected into the flowing glass if inserts are required. Shears cut it into small cylinders of a regular size and these are rounded off by mechanical rollers and left to cool. 'Machine-mades' – as they became known – proved superior for shooting, and players no longer had to compensate for eccentric trajectories. There was also a huge reduction in unit cost. American manufacturers ought really to have had the competitive edge, but sales didn't take off until the First World War in Europe cut off supplies from Germany. By the mid-1920s German marbles were no longer as prized as they had been and they were more or less finished as market leaders.

With virtually all marbles being made by machine from 1910, the next two decades proved to be a golden age. Manufacturers vied with each other to produce more unique designs and ever more colourful marbles, with exotic names such as Akro Agate Corkscrews, Popeyes, Peltier National Line Rainbows, Swirls and Peerless Patches. The Great Depression took away the shine and with manufacturers becoming more cost-conscious the more brightly coloured marbles began to disappear.

By the 1960s, virtually all marbles were made in the Far East.

A marble made of pure ground marble, or other suitable stone, is highly prized and regarded as being the most accurate for shooting. Clay marbles are cheap but tend to be irregular and dull in appearance and, although they were once the most common of marbles, lack of demand has made them hard to find. Today, marbles are made from all sorts of materials, but glass remains by far the most popular. It is the most suitable medium for machine production and provides marbles which appeal to the eye and the touch in equal measure.

The game itself has dozens of variations: marbles may be aimed at holes and dimples, through arches or at a 'jack'. One game, Ring Taw, is frequently played by adults and now has official rules, as laid down by the British Marbles Board of Control. Forty-nine half-inch-diameter marbles are used, and each player has a tolley, a larger marble of up to three-quarters of an inch. The ring, drawn on any available hard surface, is six feet in diameter. The objective is to knock more marbles outside the ring than the opposing player or team. At the start, the forty-nine marbles are compressed into a circular 'pack' in the middle of the ring. The captain of the team 'tolleys off' by holding their tolley to their nose and letting it drop into the ring. The tolley nearest to the edge of the ring plays first. Each turn starts with the tolley placed in the crook of the index finger and flicked from the edge of the ring towards the marbles inside. Every marble knocked out of the ring scores. Judgements are made by looking from directly overhead: a marble which lies exactly on the line is still in but if its middle is beyond the line it is out. If one or more marbles are knocked out and the tolley is still within the ring, the player gets another shot and his turn continues until he fails to knock a marble out or the tolley itself goes out. If a shot fails to knock a marble out and the tolley finishes inside the ring, it stays there until that player's next turn. This is to be avoided since it means the tolley can be 'killed' – knocked out of the ring – by the opposing team. A dead tolley is not removed, but the player is handicapped by having to 'knuckle down' his shots, playing them with the back of the hand touching the ground. The game ends when the last marble is knocked outside the ring and the winner is the player or team who collects most marbles.

There are many variations, with differently sized playing areas and numbers of marbles used. Other games do not use the knuckle-down rule and when a player's tolley is knocked out of the ring, that player is eliminated from the game.

That's the official version, anyway. Children displayed less formality, and though they kept to rules that were basically the same, they could set up a game anywhere there was a drain cover or a hole in the ground to aim at. And while adults would generally 'play fair' and return all marbles to their original owners, children have always preferred to play 'for keeps' with any opponent's marbles gleefully added to an ever-growing collection. Many children had pouches and bags especially tailored for collecting huge amounts of marbles.

MARBLESPEAK

DUBS — *Hitting two or more ducks out of the ring.*

DUCKS, MIGGS OR MIBS — *The marbles placed in the ring to be shot at.*

FOR FAIR — *Playing to return to owners all marbles won during game.*

FUDGING — *Moving hand across line when shooting — forbidden!*

HISTING — *Raising hand from ground in shooting — forbidden!*

KNUCKLE DOWN — *To rest knuckles on ground when shooting.*

LAGGING/DRIBBLING — *Tossing or shooting for line to determine order in which players shoot.*

LAG LINE — *Line formed by mark on ground ten feet away from lagging point.*

LOFTING — *Shooting in an arch through the air instead of rolling shooter on the ground.*

MIBSTER — *A marble player.*

PICKS — *Removing obstructions or levelling ground in front of shooter.*

ROUNDSTERS — *Taking a different position for shooting (on rings only).*

SHOOTING/FLICKING — *Holding taw between thumb and first finger and releasing it by force of thumb.*

SNEAKING — *Shooting to lay close to ducks for next shot.*

TAW, TOLLEY OR SHOOTER — *Marble shot from the hand of the player in the game.*

Another game that was just as popular at the start of the twentieth century as it had been millennia earlier was tiddlywinks. The history of the game is obscure, though it may be based on an ancient Chinese game called *t'an ch'i*. In 1906 a Cambridge academic translated *t'an ch'i* as 'tiddlywinks'. Not absolute proof of the game's provenance or its ancient Eastern origins, but it does prove that Edwardian university dons knew about the game!

T'an ch'i was played on a board by two players, each having six small discs. The exact moves are unclear, but the aim was probably to knock the opponent's discs off the board. It would only be tiddlywinks if some kind of 'squidger' was used to propel the discs. The same academic's revised 1912 translation of *t'an ch'i* was 'a kind of Chinese tiddlywinks; squails'.

The *OED* defines squails as 'a game with small wooden discs propelled across table or board' while *Webster's* says it is 'a formerly common game, now rare, in which the discs are driven or snapped'. *It's All in the Game*, a history of Milton Bradley, devotes a page to squails, calling it a 'boisterous affair' and 'the jolliest game ever invented', before proudly claiming that it was introduced to America by Mr Bradley himself in 1867, though his attempts to popularise it met with limited success.

The British firm Marchant Games told one enquirer in 1955 that they had been manufacturing tiddlywinks for over a hundred years and the Museum of Childhood in Edinburgh has an exhibit that dates the game to about 1860, the earliest hard evidence. The game was also known in many European countries: in France it is called the *Jeu de la Puce* – Game of the Flea – a reference to the way the counters jump.

The birth of American 'tiddledy winks' is clearer. In 1883 several elderly English ladies entered the Schwarz department store New York and asked for the game of 'tiddledy winks'. Since none could be found anywhere in America, Schwarz undertook to have some rather crude sets made for them. These caught on, and American games manufacturers began making them. By 1890, tiddledy winks, as American games companies like to call it, had become popular.

The rules given in the *Young Folks' Cyclopaedia* show similarities to modern tiddlywinks in that it was played on thick cloth with two or four players sitting opposite each other. Each player had six winks of the same colour. Potting was rewarded with an extra turn. An 1890 set of tiddley winks manufactured by McLoughlin Bros (later bought out by Milton Bradley) has similar rules, though the idea of getting a wink into a pot was claimed as a new feature.

90 Years of Fun, the history of Parker Brothers, describes tiddley winks as a craze that occurred in America in the 1890s and apparently the words were originally registered as a trademark, though no one knows why or when it became a generic term for the game.

While we're on enduring games from ancient times that are still around today a few words about skipping might not go amiss, since it was a universal game for children throughout the twentieth century, and for many years before that. The game had travelled a long way, from the backyards of Egyptian and Chinese rope-makers where children began to invent games with leftover pieces of rope. Travelling sailors, having seen the fun the children were having, took the idea back to their own lands. Dutch settlers took skipping games to America and they were soon copied by their English counterparts. During the 1700s the game was mainly for boys, as girls were not encouraged to be physically active in case they harmed themselves. In the 1800s boys and girls were both encouraged to play in skipping games and three types evolved: solo single-rope activities; a long rope with someone turning at either end; and double-dutch, with two ropes turning in opposite directions.

As girls became more involved in skipping during the 1900s they invented different rhythms and singing games – On a Mountain Stands a Lady, I Like Coffee I Like Tea, and so on. Another game was to count the number of kisses given by an imaginary sweetheart and went something like: 'Now now [Jenny] I'll tell your mother, kissing [Tony Smith] down by the river. How many kisses did he give you?' And then the skipper jumps to the count – five, ten, fifteen, twenty.

Skipping seems to typify childhood in the twentieth century and many of the black-and-white realist films of the late fifties and early sixties feature an almost obligatory street scene with scruffy kids skipping in traffic-free streets. But at the start of the third millennium the centuries-old pastime seems doomed by the onslaught of more sedentary, technologically advanced indoor pursuits.

The use of cutting-edge technology in toys is nothing new,

of course. Almost as soon as Teddy bears appeared they were being fitted with a gentle growl. Dolls who could manage an approximation of human speech weren't far behind. This was not as innovatory as the manufacturers made out: they'd been known as far back as the thirteenth century. Albert the Great, the Bishop of Ratisbon in the 1260s, commissioned a local craftsman to make him a doll with a talking head. While his court was amused by the novelty, others were not. Convinced that the doll was the devil's work, Thomas Aquinas, the Italian monk and scholar, tricked his way into the bishop's palace and destroyed the talkative toy. This was but one of innumerable episodes that show that dolls are more than simple playthings. Their human form gives them a significance and a symbolism way beyond their component parts of wood, rubber and porcelain. In the USA the Negro Mothers Association of Washington called for black parents to buy their children only black dolls in the hope of instilling race love, loyalty and contentment among their children. Toyshops had plenty of these dolls, but the names they were saddled with show just what a struggle such groups would face over the next century in terms of civil rights and equality. The Negro Mothers would surely never sanction dolls with names like Nigger Babies or Kaffir Jim, a supposedly comical chap made of black indiarubber who, at the squeeze of an attached puffball, poked out his tongue and rolled his eyes. Timi-Tipp, a tinplate racing game, had black boys attempting to negotiate greasy poles – a metaphor if ever there was one! In their ignorance the manufacturers – universally white in this period – were blind to the offence they were causing. So racial and national stereotypes abounded. Indeed, stereotyping seemed obligatory in the doll-making world. On this side of the Atlantic, toy-trade magazines had a world of nationalities to offer, from Irish Paddys and Colleens to a pig-tailed Dutch girl called Miss Hook of Holland and her sweetheart Jan. Scotland had its own dolls, too – Wee Wullies and Miniature Maggies. English dolls came blessed with more favoured names: Our Little Dreadnought and – many years before its equine namesake – an army-uniformed doll called My Little Territorial.

Stuffed toys were legion and their names were nothing if not a tribute to the insular and class-conscious nature of the British public: Kilted Jock vied for children's affections with Reckless Reggie of Regent Street. Less lovable but equally desirable was Kamerade, a German soldier who raised his arms in surrender; naturally there were no end of British dolls for him to surrender to, including an airman figure, complete with moustache and heavily oiled hair. And offering moral support for our chaps at the front were Stickit – a British bulldog character in a khaki cap – and Jacko, a slightly creepy chimp doll dressed in naval gear.

Cuddliness and bathos were also admirable qualities in the world of soft toys. There was Billy Owlett, a cuddly bird in red waistcoat, white trousers and blue jacket, bought by Queen Mary among many others, and Oh-My-I, a morose dog complete with hat, spotted dickie bow and eye-patch. But even in those days America could always outdo Britain in squeamish cutesiness. Say hello to the Spearmint Kidds ('the dolls with the Wrigley eyes!'), Miss Broadway and the Yankee Doodle Twins – all perfect representatives of the American WASP way of life complete with irony-free names that were the flip side of racial stereotyping.

Other dolls, long pre-dating later crazes such as Furbies and Cabbage Patch Kids, were the must-have toys of their day: the Goo-Goo Doll of Christmas 1916 and the Long-Legged Doll of 1917. The most significant development of all came not long after the end of the First World War when character merchandise began to appear: Dismal Desmond in 1926, Mickey Mouse in 1930, followed by Pluto, Goofy, Lucky Oswald, Popeye and others, mostly inspired by popular cinema figures. There was even a Charlie Chaplin doll.

While the girls played with their dolls, the boys sometimes wanted more than small glass spheres once they'd left their cuddly toys in the nursery for good.

Hope is revived in the bosoms of the females by this manly fellow (yes he's got wavy hair and the rest of it!). The beauty chorus holds

33

its breath! What a lad! What a talent! The girls gurgle in rapture and Edwin is exclaimed as if he was a matinee idol and finds as a result of his skills that he can select any one of the adoring females who watched his act to be his future wife.

Such was the potential power of... the diabolo. All this from a simple game in which players held an outstretched length of string between their hands and then tossed and caught a spinning bobbin. Roultango was a similar throw-and-catch game, with each player holding two sticks and tossing a third spinning stick to and fro between them. Spino consisted of a miniature spinning-top being placed at the top of a sloping board; as it made its way towards the bottom it collected scores. Spinning was obviously a money-spinner in the 1910s.

Miniature billiards, such a Pot Shot, was ideal for anyone who had grown tired of spinning things and didn't have the room or spare cash for a full-sized table. There was also table croquet, which hopefully did not require kiddies to drive spiked hoops into the best dining-room table. Best of all was the Cocoa-Nut Shie, a mini-version of the fairground game but played using hazelnuts – to be provided by the purchaser.

Dean's Rag Books were launched in 1903 'for children who wear their food and eat their clothes'. The first edition was one-colour, hand-printed on unbleached calico. Despite being rather expensively priced at six shillings it proved an instant success in Edwardian nurseries. The company trademark had two dogs pulling with teeth, similar to the Levi's TM. On the back of this success Dean's Rag Book Company Ltd was formed, with a base in London's Fleet Street. In addition to their rag books the company produced photograph and post-card albums, cut-out doll sheets, kites, blow-up toys and rag dolls. At the outbreak of the First World War Dean's joined with other firms in the toy industry to try and make good the shortage of imports from Germany and Austria. In 1915 their 'Kuddlemee' catalogue contained illustrations of three mohair bears and in 1917 moulded faced dolls were produced for

the first time. During WWI export editions of the rag books were produced with Russian text, but Germans arrived in Vilna the day after the first shipment arrived, so whether the books ever got to be read by anyone is unknown. John Hassall – famous for the 'Skegness Is So Bracing' poster – was one of their illustrators.

A small boy on his home-made wooden scooter, April 1916 (Mary Evans Picture Library)

While these indoor pursuits would pass the time on rainy days, children generally could not wait to get outside. And once there, they wanted to move as quickly as possible. The first crude roller-skates had been recorded as early as the mid-eighteenth century (which was nevertheless pretty slow development of the summer market as iron ice-skates in Scandinavia can be traced back to around AD 800). In 1735 London socialite John Merlin caused a considerable stir when he turned up at a masquerade party wearing a pair of skates – which he had constructed earlier in the day. Though renowned as something of an inventor, the eccentric Mr Merlin was in such a rush to show off that he'd had no time to practise the art of safe skating. Unable to control his speed or direction he ended up crashing headlong into a large wall mirror, severely injuring himself and doing little to advance the idea of roller-skating as a sensible leisure activity.

In 1819 a Frenchman took out the first patent on roller-skates. Similar to Merlin's prototype, Monsieur Petitbled's version had wooden soles, leather straps to secure the feet, and three wood/metal wheels in a row. Like Merlin's, these skates also could not be turned easily. It wasn't until 1863 that the four-wheeled skate made its appearance. James Plimpton's version had two pairs of wheels side by side, a pivoting action damped by a rubber cushion that allowed the skater to turn simply by leaning their body weight in the direction they wished to go.

Now that the skater had rudimentary control, the sport quickly caught on and in 1866 Plimpton opened the world's first-ever roller-skating rink at a hotel in Rhode Island. But the four-wheeler did not spell the end of in-line skates. In 1900 the Peck & Snyder Company patented an in-line version with two wheels, and then an improved three-wheel version, made by the modestly named Best-Ever-Built Skate Company, followed in 1910.

The rest is history.

For those children who couldn't get used to roller-skates more conventional methods such as bicycles, tricycles and pedal cars were available. Cartwright's Rajah tricycle boasted cemented rubber tyres. The firm also produced the Doris – a girl's trike – and the robust, tough, boys' Scout (almost identical to the girls' version, aside from the name). Their top-of-the-range pedal toy car was chain-driven and fitted with proper steering, a front headlamp and a raucous horn. The Horse, a tricycle fitted with an equine head, brought pedal power to that oldest of pretend toys, the hobby horse. A cross between skates and a cycle, the Skacycle was one of the earliest versions of the scooter, known more generically in those days as road racers.

The post-First World War years saw a boom in footcycles. The name was somewhat of a con, since the footcycles had no pedals, footcyclists having to propel themselves using their feet, rather like a two-legged version of the soon-to-be-popular scooter.

Envy, as much then as now, was all part of the childhood

Toys manufactured by wounded soldiers on display at a British Industries Exhibition, Victoria & Albert Museum, London, February 1916 (Hulton Getty)

experience. Two Folkestone teenagers, Will Hills (twelve) and William Watts (thirteen), were suspected of stealing scooters worth fifteen shillings and sixpence each. When the boys were tracked down their parents willingly handed back the scooters. Apologies were not enough to save the lads from a visit to court and their jackdaw tendencies were rewarded with six strokes of the birch.

Will and William would probably be in no mood for pranks for quite some time but practical jokes – or catches, as they were more commonly known – were perennial favourites. They included an ice-cream wafer packed with cotton wool, a raspberry-jam pot with a snake inside, a floating sugar cube, a snake in a camera and a box of fake chocolates. Insects have always been good to cause a panic and the Crawling Bug joke was an ideal example: 'Crawls across the supper table, piano keys or anywhere else the gentle joker cares to place him.'

Toy-makers had dozens of other devices for the prankster's arsenal of mirth: a spraying pencil, fake cigarette packets, a collapsible hat-peg and all manner of springy things which launched themselves at the unwary from pots of jam, cigarette boxes and jewellery cases. There was even a cigarette box in which all the cigarettes were joined by a fine chain, explosive ciggies, stink bombs, chilli-filled sweets and devilish powders with self-explanatory names such as Itchykoo and Ashoo!

And no joker was properly equipped without a mask. The latest Electric Masks were everything the incorrigible joker yearned for – 'Weird! Startling! Humorous!' – and he wouldn't have needed exclamation marks to sell him on the possibilities. Designs ranged from a Mephisto to a British bobby, all featuring 'electric' eyes which popped out at the touch of a hidden catch. Other variations came complete with 'electric' noses or ears, which presumably just moved to amusing effect.

No doubt the arrival of 'toy periscopes' was loosely inspired by wartime submarine activities, but the publicity wouldn't have led you to suppose so. Instead of showing brave boy submariners spotting enemy battleships prior to launching a torpedo, the adverts suggested that the most playful use would be to spy over the wall or round the corner at courting couples. It's as if the description 'toy' gave the periscope owner an excuse for all kinds of dubious voyeuristic activity.

The ongoing war brought its own kind of perverted leisure. Government departments placed orders with several British firms to supply dominoes, chess and draughts – a total of ten million sets – to be used to occupy the fighting men of Britain, France and Russia. Whether shell-shocked Tommies ever had the time for a gentle game of dominoes amid the carnage is unrecorded. Jigsaw puzzles were also chosen as therapy for the front line and were apparently much in demand by men serving in submarines, though a sailor putting together a breezy Highland scene would probably have even more reason to feel somewhat claustrophobic.

The servicemen who eventually made it back home weren't treated in any less of an ironic way. Disabled soldiers and sailors who were given employment at the Lord Roberts Memorial Workshops were taken on a sightseeing tour around Virginia Water. After being entertained to tea with Lord Cheylesmore they reportedly had much excitement from sport and games – especially a tug-of-war between one-armed and one-legged men. 'All going to cement the good feeling that exists,' noted the reporter, without a trace of cynicism.

1920s

The legend of the pogo stick dates back to just before World War One. As legends should be, it's rather far-fetched, but it's zany enough to merit repeating. The idea, so it goes, was brought back to the West by a German who'd been travelling in Burma. While lodging with a poor farmer he'd been intrigued when the farmer's daughter, Pogo, complained about having to negotiate all the mud and rocks that lay on her path to the local temple. Being shoeless made it doubly awful. The poor girl arrived for prayers looking like the loser in a mud-wrestling contest. Unable to afford footwear for Pogo, the farmer made her a crude 'jumping stick' by attaching a short crosspiece near the foot of a pole. After practising on it for a few days, Pogo became proficient enough to hop over the stones and muddy puddles on the way to the temple. Returning home to Germany, the traveller improved on the idea by attaching a spring to make the stick bounce.

True or not, it's evident that the pogo stick was making a mark in the years after World War One and that some of its origins were traceable to Germany. A US department store, Gimbel Bros, imported a shipload of German pogo sticks only to find that humidity and sea water had warped the wood, making them useless. Desperate to meet a growing demand, Gimbel turned to an Illinois toy designer to come up with a better version. The result was an all-metal pogo-stick with an enclosed spring. So popular did the craze become that the toy firm went into full-time pogo-stick production and even taught the dancers in the *Ziegfeld Follies* how to use them. The first performance in 1920 featured a marriage on pogo sticks. Chorus girls at the New York Hippodrome performed

Swedish children go wild on pogo sticks, 1922 (Mary Evans Picture Library)

whole shows on pogos. Marathon pogo contests were held, and daredevils vaulted obstacles on the sticks.

On the other side of the Atlantic, with many of the deprivations and shortages of the First World War over, toys were set to become an ever-expanding business. Around Britain, in one town or another, new toyshops were setting up at the rate of one a week. There was also a steady growth in chain stores, such as Currys, which opened two new branches – in Crewe and Shrewsbury – in the first week of 1920. Though not strictly a toyshop, Currys did much to bring affordable bicycles, scooters and pedal cars to children growing up free from the shadow of war.

Toy manufacture also provided employment for many war veterans whose physical handicaps or shell-shock prevented them finding work in mainstream factories. At the Lord Roberts Workshops for Disabled Soldiers and Sailors, ex-servicemen were able to earn a weekly wage by making all kinds of delights for British children. A portfolio of novelty games such as Hockette and Swivello took a backseat to the workshops' specialities: wheeled vehicles and hobby horses. They came with names like the Gee-Whizz-Gee, the Galloping G-G, and the Charger, which boasted lifelike movement of head and tail, 'startlingly realistic and delightfully amusing'. For the boy whose fantasy career was to be a lackey for passengers of the LNWR, the woodworking vets also produced a scaled-down porter's trolley.

In the immediate post-war years Britain could boast over thirty firms making scooters, tricycles, hobby horses and pedal cars. Their names – Auto Gallop, Auto Skiff, Aeroette, Nip-a-Long, Nipper, Little Wonder, Joy Cycle, Cherub and Kiddie-Bike – conjure up a picture of a generation of children mobilised in some eccentric convoy. The Auto Scooter was propelled by means of a pedal attached to one side of the foot-board. The idea behind this was to avoid the toil of pushing off the pavement with the foot: 'Eliminates overdevelopment of one leg and rapid wear of one boot,' the publicity crowed, attempting to soothe the worries of parents who might be on a small footwear budget. The health-and-efficiency card was worth playing too: 'Brings all-important trunk muscles into play. Children may cover long distances to school etc. rapidly and without fatigue on the Auto Scooter.' Several other firms made these pedal-powered scooters, with prices ranging from ten shillings and ninepence to a whopping forty-nine shillings and sixpence.

A similar principle was in use on the Empire Hand-Action Karts. The same lever action was used to propel the cart, but this time it was deployed by hand from a sitting position. As well as giving the 'cartist' a stick to jiggle, this 'hand-action' propulsion avoided the need to beg for a push from pals or find a steep hill. How great a speed could be achieved with elbow action alone is sadly unrecorded, but one would guess that it wouldn't give traffic policemen any worries.

Scooters had become big business and competition gave rise to some sharp jabs from the copywriters' pens. 'Who has not seen that small-wheeled scooter dilapidatedly dithering,' mocked one advert, 'instead of running smoothly like the Lines Fairy Scoot?' The quaintly named Fairy Scoot had enormous twelve-inch wheels and wired-on tyres. More luxury features came in the shape of adjustable handlebars with grips and a rubber-covered footboard. It was surely a sturdy machine, for just in case they missed a niche market of grown-ups who didn't mind making fools of themselves, adverts added that the scooter was strong enough for adults.

All manner of mutations were thrown up by the scooter craze. The Skip Scoot, for instance, combined skipping with scooting: 'An ordinary scooter with a joyous thrill!' Since the scooter wheels had been designed with off-centre hubs, 'skipping' (without a rope) while on the footboard propelled the vehicle along with an eccentric lurching motion. It was 'The most fascinating sensation ever invented,' according to its manufacturers.

The streets of Britain must have been a wondrous sight back then, graced with curious hybrids which were neither bicycle nor scooter: the Chimac Joy Cycle or the Dandy, for instance, each of which was basically an ordinary scooter with the added 'luxury' of a padded seat that stuck up from the footboard like a shooting stick. Cynics might say that it was just another way of describing a bicycle without pedals – and they wouldn't be far wrong. Those with long legs might propel themselves along without dismounting, but it was no use for shorties. No sooner had they sat down to enjoy the ride than they'd have to get up again to apply more shoe leather to the pavement. And then sit down again for ten seconds.

One of the biggest names in scooters was Lines, whose original 'Triangle' trademark was later changed to Triangtois and later Tri-ang. In addition the firm manufactured a variety of miniature cars and other wheeled toys in their London factory. These ranged from basic four-wheelers like the Nib to the Prince No.7, fancifully described as the 'Rolls-Royce of juvenile cars'. Others included the Hatcham Motor (which took its name from Lines' works just off London's Old Kent Road) and the Victory ('Some car! This is IT. This Xmas small boys will demand an auto like Daddy's'). Motoring was on an inexorable rise in the twenties and Lines' range reflected the whole variety, from the Comet racing-car to the Morris runabout: the latter could, of course, easily outpace the former, as long as its 'driver' pedalled faster. The cutely named Chums was a toy car with a dickey seat at the back.

But if toy cars were 'IT', Lines kept their options open with traditional toys such as the Sportiboy safety rocking-horse – 'with medieval trappings' – smoothed and shaped by skilled men. For a few pence under a pound, girls could acquire one of the firm's doll carriages – 'exactly like Mummy's big one'. For the smallest members of the family Lines offered the Triangtois Puddle Duck – basically four castors with a duck's head attached – for baby to ride on.

But competition from America was beginning to bite. Kiddie Kar – with its bright yellow body and jolly red wheels – was reportedly the bestselling child's vehicle in the world. One million had been sold in the USA in 1919 and the cars soon began to arrive in British toyshops. One of the Kiddie Kar's major selling points was that its wheels had no spokes, thereby eliminating the possibility of children losing a finger or two by sticking them in at the wrong moment. Lines soon caught up with this sensible innovation and most of their toy cars were redesigned with disc wheels to reduce the risk of amputation.

But British manufacturers weren't short of innovative ideas themselves. Among Lines' more ingenious products was the Kiddie Pedal Motor-car: flick a release catch, pull on the back bumper and lever upwards to turn it into a handle, and the child's toy becomes a rather splendid pushchair. Another novelty was the Tiny Tots Joy Wheel, described as 'a scream for children's parties. Quickly solves the problem, of "What can I do?" and creates continuous laughter. Banishes shyness and keeps things going with a roar.' Quite a few claims to live up to there, so what was this marvellous Joy Wheel? It consisted of nothing more complicated than a single wheel with handgrips either side of its axle, allowing children a more mobile (and slightly more literal) version of the old 'wheelbarrows' game, where a child walked on their hands while another walked behind holding their legs up in the air. It also provided an excellent way for manufacturers to use up spare wheels, not to mention the possible inspiration several decades later for cunning 'fitness' manufacturers to market the same item as the ideal way to acquire that 'flatter, toned stomach you've always wanted'.

Profit may have been the bottom line then as now, but

many of yesteryear's toy-makers also felt duty-bound to foster good citizenship. Lessons in civic duty and family role-playing were just as important as idle amusement. This philosophy was exemplified by products such as the toy builder's truck – 'just the job for helping Daddy on his allotment clearing away rubbish and stones'. There was a complete range of junior-sized garden implements – including a fork and rake with authentic sharp prongs! – as well as a toy garden roller or the Clipper lawnmower – 'an outdoors toy for the live boy'.

Young misses were not forgotten. After all, someone had to train the wives of the future. Alongside the countless dolls came toy cookers, toy mangles and a toy brush and dustpan set which boasted a free rug beater. For girls who found rug-beating too menial (and with the free beater being a mere nine inches long it would have taken a whole day to get a rug soundly beaten) there was a vacuum cleaner that came with friction noises that made it sound as realistic (or should we say as irritating?) as the full-sized article. If the claims were to be believed, it really did pick up dust and ashes.

So much for junior housewives. Though female career opportunities were still somewhat limited, working girls were not forgotten and there were many examples of small shops to provide useful training for the next generation of shop assistants. One of the best shop games, considering itself a cut above any rival, was the Peter Pan Stores. 'Not a monotonous series of sweet bottles,' it reminded potential buyers, but a marvellous array featuring replica jars and packets from all the well-known names of the day – Bovril, Ovaltine, OK Sauce and Frys Cocoa – plus a set of working scales, invoice pad, paper bags, money and a working cash-register.

Though it had previously been a steady seller among young ladies with a secretarial bent, the sales of the German-made Bing Pigmy typewriter may well have suffered in the post-war climate. Though few British people would have given a fig, post-war conditions in Germany were deplorable. Rival British manufacturers probably applauded the news that tinplate for trains and other mechanical toys had become virtually unobtainable for their former enemies. With what few metals were available, priority was given to replacing essentials such as the millions of knives, forks and teapots that the civilian population had sacrificed for the war effort. Without coal and clay, even the factories that made dolls' heads stood idle.

While the prospects in Germany were gloomy, most British toy-makers saw the twenties as an ideal time to expand their share of the home market. Having won the war, the toy manufacturers started making arrogant claims of the superiority of British toys over the German competition. 'While they may possess certain advantages in the way of colour and gaudy finish, German toys of pre-war times cannot compare in solid worth with many British toys being produced today,' opined a *Toy Trader* editorial speculating on the future prospects for domestic manufacturers. A paragraph later and the gloves come off as the pep talk turns to a tirade against 'Hun toys' and the warlike race who make them: 'No lasting benefit can result from the renewal of intimate relations with that nation,' the editor remarks. A letter in *The Times* added support: 'to resume trade with Germany does not mean that we have risen high enough to forgive, it means we have sunk low enough to prefer profit to honour'. The letter continues with poetic imagery that Wilfred Owen would have been proud to put his name to: 'From the graves of murdered women and infants, and of the soldiers who fell by the barbarous inventions that dragged even war to a lower level, there are voices that cannot be disregarded.'

'It is surprising how quickly warlike toys have gone out of fashion in Germany,' noted one returning visitor. 'Not a single firm there is advertising guns, soldiers, soldiers' outfits or any kind of warlike games.' There were even moves to ban the manufacture of toy whips on the grounds that such items did nothing but encourage brutality. But if such moves were meant to portray Germans as a gentle people they had come somewhat late in the day.

Back in Britain, meanwhile, despite the recent deaths of millions, children were having great fun with war games and

British manufacturers had no such qualms about furnishing the toys to make such play possible. What better way for children to celebrate the victory? Every aspect of the recent conflict could be re-enacted in miniature, with Whiteleys British Tanks – 'exact copies of those used in France and Flanders!' – and machine-gun emplacements. Sets of Fry's Fighting Soldiers came complete with trees, barbed wire, machine-guns and dispatch rider. On the toy front line hundreds of soldiers could be wiped out with the sweep of a juvenile hand. There was even a toy submarine that stealthily moved under water for up to fifty seconds.

Yet some German toys were still being produced and getting through, though it was usually under false pretences. Many were exported to the USA and were labelled as being made in Allied or neutral countries. Toy wholesalers who were found to be knowingly abetting this subterfuge were quickly hauled before the courts and had their stock confiscated and destroyed.

The defeated Germans turned their ingenuity to other inventions, like a device that enabled one-armed poker players to shuffle and hold cards in one hand. Terrys made a playing-card holder which clipped to the edge of the table and held cards fanwise in a coiled spring. They claimed, bizarrely, that their gadget would also be useful for those who wished to have both hands free while playing. To do what?

'Toy Slaves' were not a new line in dolls but the subject of a headline for a newspaper story about German toy workers. According to the *Daily Herald*, organ of the British Socialist Party, the 'slaves' were paid two shillings for a twelve-hour day making fancy goods and cheap nick-nacks. 'A blot on capitalist civilisation' was their term for the thousands of families from the 'decaying lower middle classes' who were engaged from dawn to midnight (a rather liberal interpretation of a twelve-hour day). The 'Made in Germany' label was an affront to humanity. Nuremberg Fancy Commodities company sold its miniature railway locos at fourpence each – yet the workers who assembled them from cut-out sheets were paid just fivepence a gross – the equivalent of a penny an hour. 'Made in

Germany' should also have said 'with the sweat and health of other children'.

With Germans out of the running, Italian toy-makers seized the opportunity to muscle in on European markets. According to one supporter at least, Italians had always rebelled against ferocious, ugly or meaningless toys – like those from Germany. Italian felt dolls were described as beautiful, unbreakable – and cheap. A variety of mannequins arrived in British shops – a sentimental pierrot, a Chinaman, Red Indian, cowboys, and a marvellously detailed brigand with a sugarloaf hat, flowing locks and stiletto knife. Yet even the Italians had their detractors. Some reports claimed Italian toy-makers had a nasty habit of covering their cuddly toys with *real* skins from bears, horses, cows, dogs, sheep and cats. Regarded as something of a status symbol in Italy and no more remarkable than a crocodile handbag, those in the British doll-making trade reported the practice with great disgust. Less expensive, less offensive and probably less smelly, too, were soft toy ducks, dachshunds, squirrels and parrots covered in harmless felt.

One dreads to think what the Italians might have used for stuffing their skin-covered cuddly toys. In Britain firms like Chad Valley now packed their soft toys – rabbits, cats, spaniels and camels – with the latest innovation in stuffing: alva marina was a dried sea grass which was sweet and clean, vermin proof and non-flammable. Another common stuffing was kapok, a cotton-like substance obtained from the seeds of a tree native to South-east Asia.

In spite of the horror stories of German slaves and Italian toy cats covered in real cat, it was felt that the British toy manufacturers needed more assistance than simple propaganda. There were taxes on lace and embroidery, blown glass – which included dolls' eyes – and the new voice-boxes. Totted up this could mean a tax of twopence on a single doll. Importers had to stump up the cash for all of these, which cut into profits. But they also had to pay the administration costs – inspection, cleaning and warehouse charges – that were needed for the collection of the taxes. On a consignment valued at thirty-four

Dolls for sale on a Berlin street. Germany was the home of toy manufacturing in the first quarter of the twentieth century (Hulton Getty)

pounds, the importer was billed eleven pence for the various taxes; however, he was also lumbered with an eight-shilling charge for the administration costs.

The war was still on everyone's mind, even those enjoying the new-fangled idea of seaside holidays. The small packs of sandcastle flags sold at railway stations, toyshops and beach stalls were pointedly exclusive, with only the Union Jack, Stars and Stripes, Belgian and French standards available. Few would have done so, but the boy who flew the German red-and-black colours from the top of his gritty citadel was likely to have the whole edifice demolished with a well-aimed boot.

The seaside had a toy culture all its own. Alongside seaside spades in eleven sizes and shapes and old-fashioned fishing-nets available to suit all budgets at one penny, twopence and fourpence-halfpenny were Happynak seaside pails and Razzle-Dazzle beach balls, painted wooden yachts with cotton sails, some with amazing detail in their brass fittings, and Bathing Jeff – a soft floating doll designed especially for the seaside. Few of these toys ever made it back to the towns and suburbs – for what use did anyone have for fishing-nets and beach balls in the back streets of Manchester or Leeds? According to the Manchester *Guardian*, LMS railway staff had to dispose of hundreds of buckets and spades that were left on their trains every summer holiday season, 'along with the dead and feebly surviving specimens from Britain's rock-pools'. Whether any of these crabs and shrimps ended up in the porter's sandwiches must remain a matter of conjecture.

If the children were receiving a grounding in botany at the rock-pools, dolls were useful in educating the young about people from around the world. Toyshop windows boasted a veritable League of Nations – a Zulu Chief, Minnie Ha-ha, a Snow Boy, and an Italian Boy (bizarrely, complete with a monkey). There was even one called the Fums Up Doll, whose head and face were spookily like that of the Yet-to-land Roswell alien. All perfect stereotypes, no doubt, but in those days political correctness was a good half-century off. Just for good measure, doll-makers could even do you a bit of classism too, exemplified by a rubberised Eton Boy doll, complete with detachable topper (for winter) or boater (for summer).

But a doll was nothing without its head. Torsos and limbs were left to any old artisan to cobble together, but the makers of heads considered themselves specialists, artists even, and a cut above. One firm, Hewitts, was most proud of its latest line – dolls' heads with sleeping eyes – though they apologised for any decline in standards brought on by the war: 'Our heads are admitted to be equal to any continental heads imported. Owing to inferior raw materials, poor labour and other causes beyond our control in the later stages of the war, these heads have unfortunately deteriorated slightly from our normal high standards.'

Many dolls' heads came from Staffordshire potteries, which had once churned them out by the thousands, neatly arranged in rows alongside the plates and teacups. Hundreds of workers depended for their livelihood on the continuing production of the heads but the trouble was pottery was fine for cups and saucers, but it had never really been an ideal medium for any-thing played with by a child. Even girls were inclined to be careless and fractured skulls were commonplace. No wonder then that the toy world warmly welcomed the invention of Noxid. This new wonder material set as hard as stone and was a much better choice than brittle porcelain. As one impressed visitor to the Noxid factory put it: 'a good hard slamming – as demonstrated to us – failed to break the doll's head'. But one factory's innovation was another's bankruptcy. Letters to toy-trade journals – mostly signed 'Worried of Stoke-on-Trent' – appealed to doll manufacturers not to put profit before the dedication of England's pottery workers.

While makers of dolls' heads were numerous, Britain had only two firms in the business of making glass eyes. One was the long-winded National Doll and Glass Eye Manufacturing Co.; the other Freemans of Birmingham, with forty years' experience and whose attention to authentic veining and cor-nering was particularly praiseworthy. For toyshops who wanted to check the quality for themselves, a sample parcel of eyes, fixed and sleeping, would be dispatched on receipt of a one-shilling cheque or postal order.

Names for dolls ranged from the cutesy predictable – Tinkles, Wobbles, Goo-Goo (with mohair wigs, china head and glass eyes) – to the bizarre monikers of the Flesho dolls – I'se All Dicky, Long Exposure and Mr Pussyfoot. Iddy Umpty, a Boy Scout signaller, came in a box complete with a set of Morse-code lessons. Who could resist Cosycuddle, 'the kiddies' cold weather friend. Her body is as unique as her face – it radi-ates warmth, is soft, comfy and squeezable, also safe. The ideal bedfellow'? Barely registering a flicker on the lovability meter was the hair-raising Scary Ann: hand-painted, she came with a tousled wig of bobbed hair which stood on end when an attached lever was pressed. From the USA came Ma Chunk, 'a fat little chunk of timely interest', and Sunny Orange Maid – not so much an ice lolly as a 'new, glowingly bright young lady'.

These names came pre-attached. But most mass-produced

dolls pre-dated *The Prisoner* by fifty years, such as the Colonial Toy Co.'s No.100, No.102, No.198 and No.201(S). All these were 'fully formed, plumb pink, washable, with baby-like bodies and sleeping eyes', but anonymous. Still, what the heck, little girls could call their dolls whatever they wanted to. There was no obligation to adopt the manufacturers' names and few girls would rush to their toy box with the greeting, 'Good morning, No.102 – what shall we play today?' Still, perhaps No.102 was preferable to the Effanbee. One assumes the name for this 'new-born baby doll' was derived from manufacturers with the initials F and B, but it was unfortunate that it sounded like a way of cursing the infant: 'You effin' b!'

In adverts other dolls proudly proclaimed their patriotism even if the names suggested a certain refugee status: 'I am British, my name is Misska, I am the prettiest doll in England.'

Dolls, pretty or otherwise, were of little interest to boys, of course, who by 1925 were embarking on a Brave New World of engineering. There were now nine Meccano sets – 1 to 7, plus the simpler 0 and 00 versions that were put together around very simple concepts for the youngest boys. Outfits 5 and 6 were optionally available in oak cabinets instead of the usual cardboard boxes, while the superlative 7, priced at eighteen pounds and ten shillings, remained beyond the reach of all but the luckiest lads. With set No.7 one could build a complete motor-car chassis, complete with working gear-box, clutch, differential and rear-wheel brakes. Whether anyone ever attempted this is unknown. The twenties also saw the intro-duction of geared roller bearings – the most complex Meccano component ever devised – rubber tyres and a boiler.

In 1926 'New Meccano' arrived, with certain parts enam-elled in red or green. Objections to the change were inevitable and purists were initially allowed to swap the coloured pieces if they so wished. But pandering to purists meant having to double up on the production line, and by the following year all sets were being issued solely in red and green. The colour changes certainly brought increased sales, but irked many Meccano loyalists who had previously constructed models to update and found they could no longer buy an uncoloured part to match.

Not that Meccano had the market all to itself. Toyshop windows had scores of similar construction sets to tempt the junior engineer. With the Kinco (set No.1) a boy could make two hundred different models, from a letter balance to a Maxim gun to an emery wheel. Erector was 'the toy like structural steel'. The Irish Toy Co. cashed in on its compatriots' skill on building sites to offer Villeto and Dometo, sets of miniature building-bricks, while Bricco, from Swan Toys, had a system of prefabricated bricks very much like the later Bayko.

But Meccano remained the biggest and had the highest profile. By 1926 Hornby had set up Meccano factories in Paris and New Jersey. A publicity picture showed Jackie Coogan – Charlie Chaplin's co-star in *The Kid* – at work on a crane that was nearly as big as himself: 'Jackie Coogan is a keen Meccano boy,' the advert proudly announced. Considering that the 'most famous boy actor in the world' was then earning $22,000 a week, Meccano seems like quite a modest hobby compared to what the twenty-first-century brat pack like to spend their earnings on.

During World War One, in common with most engineering firms, Meccano had been employed on government work, with precious little time or materials available for something as trivial as toy-making. But a very limited supply of Meccano had been produced and in 1918 there was even an innovation – the architrave corner bracket. Since this proved ideal for use as the cabside of a steam locomotive, Hornby had a rudimentary four-wheel loco built. Rather pleased by the looks and performance of the finished prototype, Hornby decided that model trains would be an ideal venture for peacetime. Soon afterwards, in 1920, Meccano announced its first Hornby trains, 'the new idea in clockwork trains'.

Their first set, consisting of an engine with gears, brakes and regulator, tender, two coaches and a circle of track, cost twenty-seven shillings and sixpence. Constructed in gauge 0, pretty much the standard scale then, the locomotive and coaches were available in a choice of LNWR, GNR or Midland livery. Unlike the printed tinplate trains made in Germany, Hornby's clockwork trains were not pre-built but sold as specialised Meccano sets, allowing locos to be constructed and dismantled. Realism was not high on the list of requirements and any mini-stoker on one of these Meccano locomotives would have had to be a long-jump champion to negotiate the yawning gap between engine footplate and coal tender.

With war reparations crippling Germany's once-powerful toy industry, British firms had the market to themselves and an opportunity to gain the edge on Continental competitors. But despite widespread anti-German feelings and a wave of 'Buy British' sentiments, Hornby knew that long-term commercial success – and his own reputation – depended on his factories being able to match the high standards set by the Austrians, Germans and Swiss. Perhaps he took his inspiration from the Eisenmann Innacircle clockwork train – which obviously was going nowhere except in a circle!

Within two years, 4–4–0 loco 2711 and its two Pullman coaches were showing far more detail and attention to realism. The train set wasn't exactly cheap at three pounds, though perhaps the routine practice of pricing items in shillings – sixty, in this case – made damage to Dad's wallet seem less severe. Soon after came the Zulus – not commuter sets from South Africa but named after a well-known Great Western locomotive. These sets were cheaper than the 2711 and came with a pre-constructed but non-reversing locomotive. The Midnight Mail set was able to collect and drop off mail sacks. Slightly less glamorous were the Hornby No.1 and No.2 'Tank Goods' sets, which included an LMS or LNER loco and a couple of 'Pratts' petrol-tanker wagons.

In 1925 came the *Hornby Book of Trains*, first in what was to become an eagerly awaited annual catalogue. As they could be picked up free from most toyshops – and usually discarded the following year – it is unsurprising that the few examples that have survived are highly prized today. By this time Hornby's

D-I-Y constructional approach had been abandoned and all the firm's locos and rolling stock were sold as ready-assembled units. Though Meccano hardliners may have been disappointed with this divergence from the company's founding principles, it was an inevitable change in reaction to an expanding market. Variety was one of the key selling points: while no one could have covered all of the thousands of companies who had their own railway wagons, Hornby offered a remarkable range. For between two and four shillings Hornby had detailed wagons and vans for Fyffes Bananas, Cadbury's Chocolate, Shell Motor Spirit, Trinidad Lake Asphalt and Nestlé Chocolate, amongst many others. Passenger coaches showed similar attention to detail, with opening doors, celluloid windows and corridor end-plates. They were bang up-to-date too, being available in the liveries of the new 'Big Four' railway companies – the LNER, LMS, GWR and Southern. The wide range of accessories included engine sheds, tunnels, platforms, signalboxes, figures and even a mini-Nestlé Chocolate machine.

One page of the catalogue featured the firm's new 00 series – trains that some suspected had been made in Germany under a secret deal. Why else would it be this one page devoid of the usual legend 'British and Guaranteed'? 00-gauge (⅛ inch to a foot) had first arrived in Britain in 1921 when Bassett-Lowke brought back a Bing miniature table railway from Germany. There were eleven sets to choose from, ranging from five shillings to thirty-seven shillings and sixpence. A typical set consisted of a 2–4–0 tank engine, two coaches, a station, a tunnel, two telegraph poles (for very short telephone calls, one supposes) and a quantity of 16mm-wide track. Though not an immediate success 00 gauge brought model railways within the reach of a mass market. An increased interest in the gauge was awakened, encouraging those like Frank Hornby to develop it.

The first electric trains had also arrived on the scene – designed to operate from a high-voltage motor and with a shocking 230 volts running through the tracks! An unthinkable risk in today's environment but the fortunate few who enjoyed electricity at that time were perhaps more aware of the dangers than those of us now who take it for granted, until it bites back.

Many toy dealers put on special model-railway displays, to which boys were encouraged to take their fathers. Hornby were well aware of the appeal to an older generation and their train sets were destined to become the ultimate in father–son bonding (or warring). By 1930 Hornby had become a household name and was used generically whether the trains were made by Hornby or not.

Trains were still frontrunners in technology at this time and were just one of several products targeted specifically at boys, who were credited with a liking for anything scientific. The firm of Gilbert offered them a choice of wireless set, telegraph set or phonograph set. There were sets to teach the principles of lighting, telephonics and magnetism, while the firm's 'weather bureau' came complete with thermometer, barometer and cloud charts. Chemistry sets were proving themselves an 'instantaneous success'. The Kingsley Chemistry Set boasted that each test-tube was hand-blown by girls in Mr Kingsley's own factory and the sets came with instructions on how to make dyes, parlour fireworks, hydrogen, oxygen and – worryingly – chlorine gas. 'A liking for chemistry is inbuilt in most boys,' said the adverts, obviously penned by a copywriter who passed away long before he could have his optimism shattered by the boys of class 3C at Burton Boys Grammar School.

Model steam engines, stationary but engineered in fine detail, were also proving themselves popular with junior engineers. Two bestselling examples were the *Miss America* and the *Peggy* – described as 'British right through', despite their names.

But boys weren't having it all their own way and girls were now making incursions into pastimes that had previously been male dominated. Fifty years before the female invasion of the media, the John Bull Printing Outfit led the way by pitching itself as a unisex amusement for would-be journalists. There were any number of variations on this theme: the Britannia Writing and Printing Set, the Empire Writing and Painting Set and the National Painting and Printing Set.

Equality, however, was still a long way off in one particular male bastion: weaponry. Production values scaled new heights in the twenties with guns like the Texas Jack (a cast-iron nickel-plated nine-incher), the Premier (a 100-cap repeater), the black-and-gold Mauser, the Deluge ('a first-rate water pistol') and the temptingly named Big Bang ('gives louder report than any other'). At the bottom of the range came the humble Tip Top, cheap at only threepence. Toy-trade papers even carried adverts for items that blurred the distinction between toys and real guns, such as Walden Alarm Revolvers, described as indistinguishable from the real thing and 'very useful for scaring burglars, footpads and dogs. No licence required.'

Air guns were another popular line. The 'happy Daisy boy' became a gun-toting role-model for a host of teenage boys, obviously happy that being seen with a decent-looking gun more than made up for being tagged with a rather effeminate name. The Ronson Revolver promised 'all the thrill, none of the danger'. There was even a workmanlike model of a machine-gun, with a flint and steel mechanism that produced a constant stream of flashes from the muzzle.

But satisfying the nation's appetite for weapons was not entirely without risks. A fierce fire at the premises of a cap manufacturer in Peckham badly scarred the faces of Rose Hebburn and Hilda Marsh, two of the factory girls.

Deliberate infernos and explosions, then as now, were reserved for the 5 November and some of the names of the fireworks were a real delight: Bengal Matches, Jupiter Candles, Emerald Cascades, Spangled Star Bombs, Ultra Violet Rays and Humming Spider. Big Terror and Little Terror were more literal descriptions of what was inside the box. Annoying people was just as much a tradition of Guy Fawkes' Night as seeing a colourful display. What pest could resist the temptation of the Sparkling Bomb, which was advertised, somewhat irresponsibly, as 'a child's delight, mother's fright'?

The market was full of pyrotechnic misnomers. Sun Electric Sparklers certainly had no connection in any way with electricity, and were simply trying to be oh-so-modern. Still, they were at least working fireworks, unlike the Everlasting Catherine Wheel, which wasn't firework at all but merely a gaily-coloured disc that the user had to spin around on a length of string stretched between the hands.

Fortunately, quieter hobbies were still going strong and there was an ever-ready market for new art forms for the country's drawing rooms. Colouring books and crayons were perennial favourites, but children eagerly seized on anything with a novel twist: Tintography – 'new hobby, new delight', Kinco Lineart Stencil, the Kinco magic pad and, as one trade journal somewhat miserably announced, 'Wet days in summer mean a steady demand for Plasticine.'

Then, as now, parents were always more willing to get their wallets out for any toy or game with a vaguely educational purpose. Kinco Plasto Map 'educates while it amuses – makes practical geography a pleasure'. The firm started off with a map of Britain first – of course – and promised other countries to follow. The maps were virtually indestructible, made on a thin steel base, with rivers of blue thread and railways of red thread inserted into the green Kinco plastic covering.

If they became bored with such thinly disguised education, perhaps children could be 'improved' through music, but little did parents know what they were letting themselves in for. How many children could resist the Hum–drummer, a far from humdrum jazz-band outfit that consisted of a triangle, drum, cowbell, cymbals, kazoo and flageolet? Enough noise-making appliances to send the most stoical parent through the entire rage range, from mild irritation to slipper-wielding tyrant. Similarly calculated to cause a breach of the peace in households up and down the country was the Drumophone, a drum and bow set. By drawing the bow across the top of the drum 'a realistic drum roll' was promised, followed no doubt by a similarly genuine cry of protest from any adult within earshot.

Girls might opt to kill two birds with one stone by demanding the Diana Musical Skipping-rope, which made a merry tinkling as it turned.

Much licence was taken with the descriptions. Musically

inclined children who pestered their parents for the Acme Jazz Junior Flute ended up with a device that was just a misleadingly named Swannee whistle – so ending any hopes of working towards a place in the National Philharmonic Orchestra. Likewise, the oddly named Musical Submarine was not a vessel full of singing sailors but 'the king of all kazoos'. Admittedly, it was shaped like a submarine, but then so is every other kazoo. The name can only have been chosen in a wild attempt to cash in on the high profile submarines had achieved during the recent war.

The Jazzith was a one-string Hawaiian guitar, but at least it didn't need any instruction book or a chord chart and it had the further advantage of being marginally quieter than a drum or trumpet, but the monotonous repetition must surely have sent parents rushing for the aspirins.

Among the multitudinous adverts for musical instruments in the *Toy Trade Journal* is one for the Jaws Harp, a twangy device intended to be held between the teeth and plucked with the finger. It makes sense, a harp for the jaw. So who corrupted the name to Jew's Harp and when and why?

Yet more noise could be created with humming tops, being trumpeted as the latest thing, with the curiously named Mozzle proclaimed as the loudest and longest-spinning of the species. The Organ had a range of ten notes and the Siren could play a whole scale. Others were even more spectacular, like the Spark, which used friction and a flint to produce a shower of sparks as it span around. There was even a model which was started up by connecting a pistol to the top and pulling the trigger.

Older children were more likely to be into kites, the craze for which was reaching new heights of sophistication. The Stunting Kite, for instance, could loop the loop and perform spiral nose-dives, and was fitted with a simple but effective device that made a motor-like buzz whenever the wind caught it.

Another innovation was the deflatable rubber ball: 'No more balls lost or stolen! Easily carried in the pocket when not playing.' This seemed like an eminently sensible idea, even if the makers had the cheek to add the claim that it 'gives additional fun by inflating and deflating' – as if it was a great lark and not a chore that might well leave the blower-upper at a serious disadvantage in any footie game that followed. Other manufacturers were even cheekier when it came to milking this simplest of ideas: the Plume deflatable ball was lauded as 'Britain's first automatic rubber ball!'

Maybe we're taking it too seriously. Throughout Britain junior lungs were busily puffing away in the cause of fun and frolics. Balloons, rather than being colourful additions to a birthday party, seemed designed to irritate. The names give the game away: Dying Pigs, Squeakers, Water Squirts, Airships. 'All Squeakers tested before leaving factory,' announced the guarantee – and it must surely have been one hell of a department to work in. Though not inflatable, the same firm's rubber beetle was described as 'a realistic creepy-crawly designed to disgust the fastidious housewife and shockable auntie'.

Balloons were not without their dangers. History records at least one fatality – a dog in Preston who died after swallowing one; a tragedy in the eyes of modern animal lovers and probably wholly avoidable. Today, if rescue was beyond the cream of TV's vets, the news would certainly have made the front pages of the tabloids. But there was no such sentimentality then, as the unfeeling doggerel that appeared in one of the toy-trade journals shows:

> To masticate a toy balloon
> The sportive doggy tried
> His breath inflated it too soon
> The dog it was that died

While real animals were mocked as they choked on rubber, their toy counterparts seemed to be more loved. They ranged from the massive to the minuscule, from Jonah's Whale to a clockwork praying mantis, with Tishy the Jumping Horse holding the ground for the more conservative. Luckily for

A German ferris wheel made of
pressed tin, circa 1910 (*V&A*); and
a toy fighter plane from the First
World War (*Robert Opie Collection*)

Early wooden tops and yo-yos; boys' gift set, circa 1910. And a very early mechanical German train set, circa 1900 (*all Robert Opie Collection*)

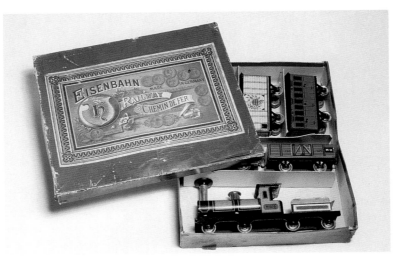

Lines fairycycle;
a grown-up version
of the Lines
fairyscoot (*V&A*)

INSTRUCTIONS for OUTFIT No. 2

The Meccano empire, which included Hornby train sets (a painted tin version of the *Flying Scotsman* at Windsor station is pictured), shaped millions of twentieth-century boyhoods (*V&A & Mary Evans Picture Library*)

Jigsaws really took off in the 1930s, replacing favourite pursuits of the twenties, like magnetic fishing. The thirties also saw early crossover merchandising, such as the Shirley Temple doll (*Robert Opie Collection & V&A*)

Boys will be boys
and girls will be girls;
timeless childhood
pursuits captured here
in the 1930s (*both Mary
Evans Picture Library*)

Look at the little 'fulkers'. Marbles,
1950s-style (*Hulton Getty*)

those who hate creepy-crawlies, the Daddy Longlegs soft toy wasn't the product of a perverse insect-loving imagination but a cuddly bunny rabbit. Somewhat more weird was Cooties, a game in which the object was to round up four 'cooties' – body lice – and entrap them in a wire cage.

Animals were expected to sing for their supper. Simple mechanisms, clockwork, rudimentary voice-boxes, had given them a new range of talents with which to delight children. Enter the walking and talking Charlie Chick, the walking and dancing Wilfred Rabbit, and Dandy Dobbin, a mechanical horse whose talents appeared to be limited to opening his mouth. Moving mouths were simple enough, but Bruno the Growling Bear emitted a vaguely ursine grunt. There were all sorts of other mechanical gimmicks, like Moovie, the pet cow that came back to a child when pushed away, and Growler, a big cat of uncertain parentage that was fixed to wooden rockers and growled as it oscillated. Moving heads were also common and a firm by the name of Beavis offered elephants, rhinos, chickens and swans, all in polished wood with nodding movements. Strangely enough, toy animals which shook their heads were very rare.

Lucky Jim and Gay Dog were soft-toy animals that did more than nod their heads. They flew across the Atlantic in the company of flight pioneers Alcock and Brown.

Even more popular was Dismal Desmond – a spotty soft-toy dog with a gloomy mien, 'its lost look wins a pity akin to love. Seldom has there been any new line which has created such a furore as this woebegone specimen of the toy designer's art.' His name became a popular foxtrot song and Desmond was soon the star of several pantomimes, comic strips and weekly film cartoons. Percy Chapman, England's cricket skipper, had Dismal Desmond as a mascot, given to him by the editor of the *People*. Did the kindly Wigan man take him in the belief that a dog so named could be happy nowhere else? After the team's victory in the Ashes, Dismal Desmond went missing in the ensuing celebrations. Chapman sent a telex to the newspaper:

'Many thanks for dog. Stolen in pandemonium last night. Very much appreciated gift. Can you possibly get duplicate for wife? – Chapman'

Animals were also a central feature of many other toys and games. From Scotland came Cat and Dog Life, a simple mechanised tableau on which a turn of the starting-handle at the side caused a loose-legged, dangly jawed bloodhound to move across in pursuit of a frightened cat. Pre-dating TV's *Pet Rescue* by seventy years came Ding Dong Bell, in which a warm glow came from being the one who would help the poor cat out of the well.

Television, of course, was a long way from becoming the surrogate nanny for the nation's youth, but radio was already being greeted with joy by some and dire warnings by others: 'Has wireless killed off card games?' asked one newspaper. Probably not, judging by the variety of old favourites and novel variations available: Snap, Gipsy, Cheery Families, Cavalry, Peter Pan, Jungle Jinks, Animal Grab, Bread and Honey, Old Maid – all described as 'card games that never grow old'. But the influence of wireless was certainly being felt: 'Exploit it!' advised the toy-trade press. Some already were: there was Radio – the wireless game – not to mention Dandy all-steel telephones which really worked.

The Electric Fishing Game seemed an attempt to bridge the gap between ancient and modern: a spare bath or a washbasin was all that was needed for 'hours of fun'. Fill up with water, then get fishing: each fish – red salmon, blue trout, silver carp, and so on – had its own score and the player with the highest total took the title of champion angler. Though the game included a blue bag (for clouding the water) there were definitely no batteries. Quite why the game was described as electric is a mystery but as there was no Trades Description Act to trouble enthusiastic traders they could call it whatever they liked. 'Electric' was something of a buzzword at the time and – if called to defend the use of the word – firms were not above saying it was meant purely as a synonym to describe an exciting sensation.

Radio may have been making its way into the better-off homes but it was cinema that was all-pervasive in the toy world. Children wanted all kinds of toys based on the movie stars of the day, while Wonder Pocket Cinema offered a selection of thirty films in penny packs. Acting out scenes from films, as children were wont to do, inspired a new craze for playsuits: Indians, Yankiboy, Tom Mix cowboy suits – as worn by the film star – or 'popular screen artist', as the phrase was then. Did children use their imagination more in those days? Even the most modest accessories were enough to please some of them: one of the big crazes of 1925 was Harold Lloyd glasses.

Crazes were not limited to the current favourite film star and could pop up from anywhere. One of the biggest sensations at the 1925 Wembley Exhibition was the Springo boomerang. Constructed from specially prepared plyboard, the boomerang was placed in a spring release mechanism from which it flew out and – hopefully! – returned. The set came complete with spring and four boomerangs: it was all 'Splendid training for the eye.' The manufacturers also offered a Special Xmas box containing eight boomerangs and a target – a cockatoo on a spring. Meant as an indoor game, they said that on still days it could be used outside. 'Performs same as actual full-size boomerang. As used by Australian blacks,' trumpeted the box lid. But, one might ask, if it worked why did one need more than one boomerang?

One manufacturer of toy soldiers and animals – Britains – hedged their bets by displaying two constrasting tableaux at the Wembley Exhibition. For the forward-looking they had the Arcadian Peace, featuring windmill, farm carts, milk churns and animals, while for those who still hadn't got over the thrills of combat they were exhibiting War, a strife-torn landscape featuring a full complement of soldiers, tanks, trenches and gun emplacements.

Far more alarming than any display of weaponry, perhaps, was the Popping Optic – also known as Wembley Eye – a monocle with an eye that could be pumped up from an attached puffer.

The Wembley show's royal approval did a great deal to help British industry, but toy firms had never been slow in exploiting a connection with the highest in the land. Caesar, for instance, was a cuddly toy dog which was supposedly based on one of King Edward VII's favourite pets. Elsewhere, newspaper adverts featured the latest Prince of Wales playing Tooty, a fortune-telling game that somehow never had the same mystic ring about it as Ouija or Tarot.

Manufacturers didn't take kindly to interference from do-gooders who expressed concerns about the safety of toys and the cleanliness of materials used. 'A celluloid bogey,' said one of the toy-trade magazines, pooh-poohing tests by the Institute of Hygiene following concerns about the suitability of celluloid in the manufacture of toys. Hadn't such toys been sold for the past twenty years without incident?

But there were always some people who reacted more quickly to the public mood. In addition to their clean-sounding 'peaches and cream' complexions, Kuddly Animals were advertised as 'sanitary, scrubbable and really unbreakable'. As the *Daily Mirror* proclaimed: 'The long reign of the ugly and the grotesque in children's toys may be coming to an end.'

At the Wembley Exhibition and in the toyshops there was no end of games with bizarre names: Krom, Milat, Bamrang, Nelsonics, Tancs, Pax, Jerke, Purzeli, Bombo, Wedding Bells, Biff Ball, the Little Sportsman, Blind Pig, Diver's Luck, Bazi, Sinnet, the Down Mail and the Weird Game. Whatever they were all about (hardly any have survived), it's odds on that some were played with the aid of Twiddlers – described as 'the exciting new idea in dice' even though they consisted of nothing more innovative than simple hexagonal pieces of card with a stick through the centre, with each section being numbered one to six.

The twenties provided a host of indoor 'sports' games, all requiring various degrees of exertion. Steeplechase, the Jockey and the Whip were all ideal choices for anyone who liked the sport of kings, while those who could see little point in horses chasing round a track unless they could stake some money on them were also catered for by the Gee Wiz Racing Game, which featured horses in parallel grooves, rather like the games that still survive in seaside arcades today. Soccer fans had the Goalie – a variation of which was later to enjoy huge popularity as Subbuteo. There was even an Egg and Spoon Race, though quite why anyone would need to buy a pre-packaged game when most households could conjure up a few eggs and spoons is a mystery.

Anyone with a decent back garden or large living room could set up a game of Katta Skittles or Katta Bowls, both of which featured balls launched from spring catapults. Goldfish must have quaked in their bowls every time anyone suggested a match!

For parents strapped for cash or those who simply relished a challenge, the *Daily Mail* started its weekly feature 'Toy-making at Home'. When Mum wasn't beating hell out of a dusty rug, she could get out her sewing box and set to making 'delightful dolls with the simplest of materials such as old towels, handkerchiefs and buttons'. And if Father wasn't too busy down on his allotment he could no doubt fashion whole platoons with the aid of his penknife and a few sticks of wood.

Another source of toys for poorer children was the rag and bone man, many of whom toured town and city streets offering cheap novelties like flags and windmills in exchange for household waste. Children may have been over the moon to get these toys, but adults – those in official quarters at least – expressed concern about the considerable risk of disease from all the detritus piled up on the back of the carts. In some towns councils passed by-laws to outlaw the exchange of toys for rubbish. One devious Steptoe in Liverpool tried to dodge the rules by redefining his offerings as 'useful objects', such as glass bangles and looking-glasses. Magistrates took a different view of it after council officers convinced them that anything a child played with was, by definition, a toy. The hapless Scouser was found guilty as charged and fined forty shillings. In Bradford another rag and bone man was fined one pound with eight shillings costs for swapping toys for rags. He'd tried to dodge the law by dispensing his gifts from a sack instead of from the back of his vehicle, but the police had pulled him in anyway.

Oddly enough, in spite of the Liverpool magistrates' pronouncement, there was no commonly agreed definition of what a toy was. It seems it could be anything and everything, depending on the legislative thinking of the time. The Trade Board (Toy Manufacturing) Order of 1926 amended the previous loose definitions to whatever suited the collectors of taxes and levies. As the law stood then, a toy was 'any article made for sale as a plaything for children – e.g., metal toys, wooden or other hard toys, soft and other stuffed toys, dolls, children's books made of textile material and requisites for table games'. Thrown in for good measure were Xmas crackers, Easter eggs and toy musical instruments. Any part of such toys – paste, nails, screws, nuts and hinges – was also defined as a toy if they had been assembled – and just in case anyone wondered what 'assembled' meant, an extra clause explained that it was the 'putting together of parts in such a way that they cannot be separate afterwards without breaking'.

Play outfits such as cowboy suits and nurses' uniforms were defined as clothes. Dolls' heads, if exclusively made by a pottery, 'were also excluded in the legal definition of toys. Bats and balls were only toys in certain circumstances, such as when made for sale mostly as a child's plaything, and certainly not when sold to the leading lights of the village cricket team.

Children remained blissfully unaware of all these linguistic and legal niceties, but it obviously mattered to people somewhere. At the end of the day, toys were just another taxable commodity.

1930-45

'WHO'S FOR LEIPZIG?' So ran the headline on a twelve-page extra section in the *Toy Trade Journal* announcing the Leipzig Toy Fair of 1930. Those who answered, 'Me' were entreated not to mention the war lest it spoil the revitalised trade between Britain and its erstwhile enemy. It was no jaunt for a Little Englander, for here they were all gathered, the toy-makers of Europe: the Volkers and the Vogels, the Schmitts and the Schmidts, all back in business and setting up their stalls alongside Herren Kraus, Schwarzkopf, Zimmer and Muller.

The Germans had already got the hang of this not-mentioning-the-war idea – or so it appeared. How else would they have the brass neck to market a scale model of the *Mauritania* – an Allied ship which had been torpedoed by the German Navy in 1915 with considerable loss of life?

Back in Britain there were still many who abhorred trade with the former enemy. It wasn't just that those doing business with Germans and Austrians were putting money in their pockets and reinvigorating their economies; more disgracefully it meant turning a blind eye to the needs of Britain's disabled ex-servicemen. Unable to return to their former jobs in mines and on Britain's farms and railways, many of them had found work making toys under the auspices of the St Dunstan's charity: 'No goods could be more genuinely British than those made by our war-blinded.' Patriots may have fell for calculated appeals such as this, but many of Britain's toy retailers were more hard-nosed. They felt obliged to offer their customers the best toys available – and if that meant going for acclaimed German workmanship, so be it. Some toyshop owners even stooped low enough to question the quality of toys made by men who couldn't see.

At the cinema, Disney's *Snow White* was being hailed as a 'Technicolor masterpiece!' Movie tie-ins were already big business in the toyshops of Britain and America. From Gainsborough and British Gaumont, as much as from Hollywood, the movies now had a firm grip on all areas of popular culture. A wide range of toys and games was invested with added movie glamour, from Film Star jigsaw puzzles featuring the likes of Moira Shearer and Rudolph Valentino, to Talkie Film Transfers starring the Bruin Boys.

Following close behind the first Charlie Chaplin dolls and Dismal Desmond soft toys came a host of other familiar faces. Mickey and Minnie Mouse figures, for instance, were cleverly jointed and easily bent into hundreds of amusing attitudes using the patented 'Evripoze' system. They came in eight sizes, priced from one and six to fifteen shillings to suit all budgets. 'They will beat all toy sales records,' manufacturers promised. But it wasn't just dolls – there were Mickey Mouse pencil cases, musical boxes, money boxes, fancy-dress outfits, clockwork tin toys. Even toy train-makers were getting in on the act: Lionel rushed out a Mickey Mouse Circus Train, complete with cardboard figures and the eponymous rodent starring as a circus barker. Popeye was another early cartoon hero and the Fisher-Price Popeye pull-toy in which the spinach-addicted sailor rang a bell with a mallet was one of the earliest toys licensed by the King Features Syndicate, a small American company that was destined to play the central role in most future toy merchandising.

Children's play was increasingly inspired by films and they wanted to act out the same stories they'd seen on the screen. They demanded the same clothes and accessories as their heroes, like the Wornova playsuits inspired by Hoot Gibson, a popular cowboy from the movies. Cowboys and Indians was already a standard role-playing romp, and children seemed happy enough to fight for either side, so there were also Big Chief Indian playsuits – specially designed to 'save clothes suffering in childish romps' – and tepees.

Obviously the child dressed up as Big Chief Indian was asking for trouble and there would have been no shortage of playmates ready to take pot-shots at him as toy guns remained a perennial favourite. Some were made by the appropriately named US company the Savage Arms Corp. Advertised as 'Just like Dad's', guns, especially in America, were regarded as just another way of passing manly virtues down the generations. Boys were actively encouraged to indulge their 'inborn trait of human nature', and some of the toy guns even came with ammunition – small wooden balls or Bakelite pellets: 'Sister's kitten may be stalked without tragic consequences. No danger to Mother's lampshades!' Quite what Tiddles would say about having his backside peppered with Bakelite pellets can only be imagined... Targets aren't us, perhaps. All very Just William, but it's the kind of play that would be viewed with horror these days, and it was certainly not harmless fun then. At least one British boy lost an eye due to another's recklessness with an airgun. The father of the blinded boy sued and won £125 damages. Commenting on the case, the *Evening Standard* remarked on the 'large class of people, sound in heart certainly but less so in head, who give their children airguns, bows and sharp arrows, fireworks'. Although the gun had been bought as a present by the culprit's mother, as the law stood in those days her husband was still responsible for his wife's lack of judgement.

But target practice of one sort or another seemed firmly entrenched as every boy's birthright. Toy catalogues were packed with shooting and throwing games such as the Flying Fool – who was shot 150 feet from a gun and thereby 'teaches boys the principles of aviation' – and Bristle Archery – with targets and arrow tips covered with an early version of Velcro. The same principle was also found in a darts version called Bris-Targ. Air-O-Shoot was a clever variation on the sling-shot, with the missile being returned to earth with a small parachute. There was even a Zulu Blow Gun – a game based on 'the blowpipes used by aboriginal tribes'. Whether anyone was enthusiastic about the companion Cannibal game is unknown but there was something of a fascination at this time for exotic cultures. 'Exact copies' of costumes worn by pirates, Gypsies,

Spaniards and Mandarins were all available. Exactly what kind of games called for a walk-on Spaniard or a junior-sized Mandarin can only be imagined.

While boys throughout the land were being inspired by the scenes of derring-do they saw on the cinema screen, occasionally the moguls borrowed from the kids. The Unda Wunda, a toy clockwork submarine produced by Sutcliffe Pressings of Leeds, proved so popular with children that Walt Disney Productions used it as a prototype for the submarine in their film version of *20,000 Leagues under the Sea*.

While most people picture the thirties as a time of grubby-kneed boys playing Cowboys and Indians in the street, the decade also witnessed the emergence of a plethora of indoor games. No one's carpet or table was immune from being commandeered as a play area. Chad Valley offered Escalado 'race-course on a table' or Soccaloo table-football. The increasing popularity of golf was reflected in a host of toys: Carpet Mini-golf, Winton Midget Golf and the Tri-ang Midget Golf Course. Another popular game at the time was bagatelle, something like a manual version of the later pinball machines. Players had to pot balls on to a gently sloping wooden board which had indents and semicircles of nails to mark the scoring places.

Some of the ideas were a shade preposterous. Where was the sense in spending sixpence on a set of four shove ha'penny discs? It rather defeated the point of what was intended to be a cheap, improvised game.

Britain still suffered from its Puritan past. Having too much fun could make some people feel uneasy. If toys could be redefined it could ease the guilt and many of these 'sporty' toys laid great emphasis on their use as 'training aids'. The Vivavol, a ball on string to be batted between two players, and the Kum Back series (tennis trainer, golf trainer and skittle tennis, all featuring a ball on a length of elastic) were advertised in this way, rather than as toys. Gardminton – badminton for the garden – worked on the same principle and featured a shuttlecock on a twenty-foot cord: 'all the thrills of badminton coupled with exhilarating and health-giving exercise!'

Slightly more unusual was the Be-T boxing ball. Touted as wonderful training for young pugilists, the Be-T necessitated wearing a headband and attachment from which a punch ball was suspended on a string, dangling there waiting for the would-be boxer to give it a good thrashing.

There were lots of hybrids, too: Snuka Darts – Great Britain's two favourite games combined – 'the great new game that's sweeping the land'. Another was Tiddlytennis, where counters were flipped over a net on to a specially printed green cloth. Made by the London Magical Company, the box showed Norman Long, allegedly a famous BBC entertainer, enjoying a game before going on air. In Shelvo – a popular indoor game like a cross between tiddlywinks and shove ha'penny – the object was to land metal discs on shelves. The game was advertised as 'suitable for small rooms, clubs and institutions' – though the makers were careful not to specify what kind of institution.

Such games must have seemed quaint even in the 1930s, though. Motoring and air travel fired the public imagination, and toyshops, as usual, reflected all the social trends.

Stop and Go was hailed as the first-ever traffic-lights game: the object was to visit various places in London with traffic-lights being the penalties along the way. The clockwork-driven Fares Please Bus had a red-faced conductor who ran up and down the upper deck collecting fares and making satisfying ching-ching noises with his ticket machine. Other transport toys included the Jolly Boys Charabanc and the Right-Away Train. Boys with more humble ambitions would probably opt for the Thistle, a toy milk float complete with a crate of white-painted wooden bottles.

Dizzie Lizzie was the world's only dancing auto: 'You'll laugh your heads off when you see her. The car is covered with side-splitting sayings that will make you roar: Watch Me Shimmy, Home James, A Rattling Good Time Was Had By All, Use No Hooks.' With the growing popularity of motoring, even AA and RAC patrol scouts were being marketed as play figures to get children's imaginations racing.

It was a time when airships were still glamorous and, with no one foreseeing the R101 disaster, boys excitedly made models of the prototype R100 to suspend on strings in their bedrooms. Some looked even further ahead, to rocket ships that propelled them through space powered by nothing but friction sparks. Out on the streets or the common, one could play with the Glider, a motorless aeroplane launched from the ground with a gigantic rubber band. It was capable of loop-the-loops and (note the careful wording) could reach a height of 'up to 100 feet'.

Someone who did climb considerably higher than a hundred feet was Amy Johnson, who took two 'lucky mascots' on her pioneering 1930 flight: a Mickey Mouse and – perhaps a less obvious choice as a morale booster – the ubiquitous Dismal Desmond. Perhaps when Ms Johnson landed in Australia the locals could have hailed her with the Princess Elizabeth doll. Dressed as in her official royal portrait, the doll was certain to challenge Dismal Desmond in popularity. This blatant attempt to cash in on the Royal Family didn't meet with much favour at Buckingham Palace. One British firm had previously requested formal permission to make the Elizabeth dolls, but since the Duke and Duchess of York were against the idea, the proposal was dropped. At the same time foreigners – Germans included – were making the dolls with impunity and couldn't care less how many Windsors they upset. Faced with this unfair situation, the Duke and Duchess relented and royal approval was granted: if the Windsors were going to be exploited it may as well be by British firms. Dressed in organdie and silk, with white shoes and a pearl necklace, the doll reproduced 'as nearly as possible the dainty charm of England's own dainty princess'. With a price fixed at one guinea, the doll was intended to be sold 'within the means of average people'.

But this royalist adulation didn't cut much ice with republicans and socialists. In a piece headed 'Marx in the Nursery', *The Times* reported the views of one Mr Popov who alleged that Russian children were being perverted by toys. Despite being nearly twenty years into their brave new Soviet world, children were reluctant to join in. The dolls they wanted to play with were not proletarian folk in angelic or heroic poses, but attractive figures of the Tsars, along with their carriages, footmen and guards, dressed in the attire of the nobility. Popov was concerned because children would come to see the malignant bourgeois world as elegant and romantic, populated by kindly capitalists. Soviet toys should have revolutionary themes, turning the nursery into a fit place for a Marxist child to live. As well as plays, books and films, censors should be under orders to examine every picture or toy likely to fall into a child's hand. *The Times* was duly horrified: 'Mr Popov's world would be a drab place for children, even children condemned to live in Moscow, that most drab of all capital cities.'

Described simply as a 'tousle-headed unkempt gentleman', the advertising for golliwogs made no mention of colour. While the idea of having a black doll with such a name would never be accepted today, it is obvious that the golliwog was an object of great affection for the white children of Britain. The character was the creation of Florence Upton, an American artist living in London, at the end of the nineteenth century. Her views on racism are not known, although the character she created and which became so popular in Britain during the 1930s would subsequently be described as 'an ugly caricature' by black civil rights groups. It would also be used in racist imagery by various far-right groups several decades later, as immigration from the Caribbean to Britain increased. Of course, many members of these groups would have been children in the 1930s.

Equally, if not more, offensive were the Zuzu and Dudu Nigger dolls. Another one in the same range, the Irene Mama, was available as a mulatto – an early example of 'looks to order' genetic engineering for those who may have

Animals on wheels began to appear in people's homes in the 1930s
(Robert Opie Collection)

felt that an African wasn't a suitable toy for their girls. It would be interesting to know how many white dolls were being sold and played with in Africa and Asia, and to what extent they were made into caricatures.

Less controversial was the toy sensation of 1930, Krazy Zoo – interchangeable animal toys so that zebras could be given giraffes' necks, elephants could have lions' heads. One wonders how many of America's current genetic engineers first mixed and matched animals in this way. The box of Krazy Zoo spoke of the the 'educational advantages' of the toy.

How much nicer to stick with faithful pets such as Mr Biscuit and Mr Bones, toy dogs with a pedigree, or even soft toys like Flip the Frog or Languid Lila, the indolent pussycat! Animals of all sizes and breeds were perennial favourites: from Britain's small-scale Zoological Series to child-sized horses, from donkeys to dachshunds there was always someone who wanted a fluffed-up button-eyed version of the real thing – with no food bill or poo to clean up. Who could resist Beauty the fox-terrier, Neddy the donkey, Tony the horse and Tinker the Shetland pony? Quite who thought up Tony as a horse's name is unknown, but it wasn't quite as odd as Wriggling Wizard – not a snake but a faithful-looking Alsatian. Pedigree also had a series of dogs on wheels, including an Aberdeen terrier, and a St Bernard, plus a cute-looking lamb and a Shetland pony.

Kangaroos seemed to be enjoying an unusually high profile. In addition to the Dorco inflatable Kangaroo – used as a mascot for the Australian cricket team – boys and girls alike were offered Kangru Springshus – shoes with springs on the soles which fastened to feet like skates. 'Jump, bounce, walk, dance, gives hilarious amusement!' promised the ads, adding a footnote for puritans who might think that too much fun was an affront to the Lord that Springshus were also 'an ideal muscle developer and exerciser'.

By 1932 there was a simplest-ever Meccano to encourage the tots – No.000, while the almighty No.7 set had increased its price tag to twenty-two pounds and ten shillings. A range of 20- and 6-volt motors was available, driven from the same transformers as supplied for the Hornby train sets. Following on from the suggestion of one *Meccano Magazine* reader, 1934 saw the introduction of flexible plates, perforated on the edges only, to give models a much more solid and realistic appearance. After all, a perforated ship would hardly have satisfied anyone with a yen for realism.

Sets were then resequenced as A to L. Outfit A could be used to build ninety-eight different models – everything from a pushchair and a wheelbarrow through to a wringing machine and an anti-aircraft gun. Outfit B could provide such exotica as a teacher's desk, a dentist's chair and a hawker's cart.

The *Meccano Magazine*'s editors were constantly calling for news of readers' own inventions and one in 1938 built by a Dr Axel Saugman was a powerful arc lamp that was used to treat patients with tuberculosis.

Hornby model railways were growing in popularity. Though still mostly 0-gauge, Hornby were moving away from clockwork towards electrical power, made safer and more accessible with a 20-volt transformer. It came with dire warnings against plugging the railway directly into the mains. By now virtually every aspect of the real-life railways was available in miniature – locos, trucks, signalboxes, stations, level crossings, plus luggage and platform trolleys, benches, pillar boxes and a workman's hut complete with brazier, coal shovel and poker.

Realism was not initially Hornby's strong point: take, for example, the weird 0–4–0 engines which, as any trainspotter will gladly inform you, are rare things indeed and even if they existed they would never be seen on passenger duties but just shunting an odd coal truck up and down the sidings. A working steam engine had featured in the 1928 catalogue and Hornby still harboured the idea of having authentic steam power on his track layouts, but the technicalities proved too difficult and the idea seems to have been abandoned, although it was still suggested until the 1935 catalogue.

At London department store Gamages, the Robot Railway ran throughout shopping hours, from 9.30 a.m. until 6 p.m. It had eight trains, passenger and freight, all running to a properly timetabled service around 1,000 feet of track. Fathers and sons made special trips to the shop just to look and in the weeks preceding Christmas the feature attracted hundreds of people every day, many of whom were so fascinated that they needed a gentle push to get them out at closing time.

In 1935 the Trix Company, formed by Stefan Bing and his son Franz, produced an 00-gauge railway system. The mid-1930s saw models and track in 00/H0 scale by Marklin, Trix, Hornby and Lionel. 00 meant 19mm gauge (⅛ inch to a foot scale) and H0 meant 16mm gauge (⅛ inch to a foot scale). Competitors used opposing terms, probably to scare their customers into sticking with one manufacturer. Bassett-Lowke fully supported the new system and when Hitler began to make things impossible for Germany's Jews, the company helped Bing and others find refuge in the UK. Hornby's famous Dublo series – 'the perfect table railway' – was launched in 1938 and was available either in clockwork or electric. It was destined to become as successful as Hornby's Meccano and Dinky brands and 00-gauge soon superseded the larger designs.

Trains were becoming more true to prototype in the larger scales, and individual makers used the toy gauges as a basis for producing models to scale. The scales used with each gauge varied, most makers rounding scales up or down, which has resulted in some very odd combinations, some of which continue today. Z0 gauge (24mm) was a European scale between 0 and H0. The first manufacturer was the Czechoslovakian firm Lastra; it had vanished by the mid-1950s.

Triangtois – now trading simply as Tri-ang – introduced its 'Minic' tinplate series of a hundred different models, some of which featured electric lights for extra realism. The company had the advantage of owning Hamleys, Britain's biggest toyshop and something of an institution. Founded in 1760, it had been bought by Lines, the Tri-ang parent company, in 1931.

Introduced by Meccano in 1933, Dinky Toys were originally known as Modelled Miniatures. The range initially focused on tiny mechanised vehicles such as tractors and cranes, intended to add realism to any roads and working scenes on a model railway.

Also introduced in 1933 and intended to complement the Elektron electrical outfits were Hornby's Kemex Chemistry Sets, 'hours of fascinating fun' with which a boy – always a boy – could make inks and dyes, and bleach fabrics. 'Sound method lessens the risk of accidents,' promised the adverts, though no method is that good if a boy takes no notice of it. It's not hard to imagine the ructions caused in households up and down the country when boys started playing with inks and dyes. Suggested projects included testing foodstuffs for impurities, analysing air and water quality, growing crystals and formulating invisible inks. The sets came complete with a spirit lamp, though the more expensive sets boasted a proper Bunsen burner.

But Kemex and Elektron did not prove particularly successful, probably because of strong competition. Lotts, famous for their building-bricks, also marketed a chemistry set and an electricity set – and there were dozens of similar sets on the market. All the same, it certainly shows how children were encouraged, and perhaps even trusted.

In September 1936 Frank Hornby died after an operation – a demise received 'in that great and wonderful country called Meccanoland with deepest regret'. So wrote Roland, his eldest son and the 'first Meccano boy', who now took on this great and sacred trust. Praising his father's achievements, he emotionally recalled that 'wonderful evening when he helped his father cut out those very first strips of Meccano from a sheet of copper'.

Meccano wasn't all macho bolts and girders and exploding test-tubes. Hornby also produced the Dolly Varden Dolls' Houses, collapsible detached houses made of leather board. A range of toy furniture was available, for bathroom, bedroom, kitchen and dining room.

Diabolo was still around, and in the thirties was joined by Hi-De-Ho, a very similar game for two players, the object of which was to catch a spinning wheel between the prongs of what looked remarkably like an oversized tuning fork with a wooden handle before sending it spinning back to the other player. As it said in the London *Evening Standard*, 'you have to keep on trying and trying until you are fully expert'.

On a similar principle, but slightly easier, was the longer-lived Klick-Up, which was still around in the sixties. Described as a 'first-class seller – sure-fire winner', this one-shilling toy could be played solo or with an opponent. The object was simply to catch the ball flicked up out of its cone by a steel spring.

But an even bigger craze was looming...

Previously known by several fancy names – bandalore, quiz, emigrette, incroyable and joujou de Normandie – the yo-yo had been around for centuries. It had been noted by travellers in the Orient and travelled back to Europe with them. An eighteenth-century painting of the future King Louis XVI as a boy shows him playing with his emigrette. Another name for the toy was the Coblenz, this being the city to which many French aristocrats fled, taking with them their glass and ivory yo-yos.

It's ironic that a man who invented the parking meter, ruination of so many people's enjoyment, should also be the patron of the yo-yo. The craze began when Donald Duncan spotted a Filipino waiter at a Santa Monica hotel amusing guests with his handcrafted yo-yo. The waiter had already begun to make them as a sideline when Duncan offered to buy him out. Though Duncan is credited with popularising the yo-yo, it is probably one of the oldest toys known to mankind: the Chinese had them, made of ivory with silken cords, and the Greek versions were fashioned from terracotta.

Duncan's demonstrators, in trademark white cardigans, went from town to town, working two yo-yos at once, making everyone believe they too could be champs. The word itself was trademarked in 1932, forcing competitors to call their versions

Royal Return Tops, Whirl-a-Gigs or Cheerios. But legal tussles over the validity of the trademark were destined to go on for another thirty years before in 1965 the Federal Court of Appeal ruled that the word had become so much part of the language that any attempt to keep it as a trademark was doomed. Duncan's company, drained by the legal expenses of fighting its corner, went bankrupt. The name and goodwill were purchased by Flambeau Products, who carried on manufacturing and selling the yo-yo with the Duncan name. National Yo-Yo Day – 6 June – was chosen in honour of Donald Duncan's birthday.

The first plastic yo-yos didn't arrive until 1957, previous to which they had been maple, ash or beech.

In 1968 political activist Abbie Hoffman was accused of contempt of Congress when he 'walked the dog' to entertain the House Subcommittee on Un-American Activities that was investigating his alleged sedition. Hoffman, one of the leading lights of the anti-capitalism movement of the sixties, no doubt was less enthusiastic about playing one of the other toy sensations of the 1930s (and virtually every decade since).

Monopoly wasn't an entirely original idea. The game had originally been conceived at the turn of the century by a Quaker named Lizzie Magie. She dubbed it the Landlord's Game and intended it as the perfect way of teaching people the evils of land-grabbing and property speculation. Ironically, it was the stock-market crash of 1929 that was instrumental in making Monopoly famous. The lives of millions of Americans had been devastated by exactly the same kind of speculation and exploitation that Lizzie Magie was trying to highlight, but a new version of her game helped one man overcome the effects of the slump.

For Charles Darrow, a former heating salesman, the early 1930s were one long and fruitless job search. He kept his head above water by taking any odd jobs he could find – repairing electric irons, tackling D-I-Y jobs, even walking dogs. To pass the idle hours and take his mind off his worries, Darrow made his own jigsaw puzzles, devised a combination bat-and-ball as a beach toy, and designed a pad for scoring rubbers of bridge. But nobody was willing to pay him for his troubles.

Darrow's situation was hardly unique. Most of his friends were out of work, too. Movies, theatre or any entertainment which cost money was beyond their reach, so in the evenings they got together and talked about the better times they'd known. Darrow often reminisced about the comfortable life his family had led just a few years before and their annual holidays in Atlantic City. It would be the famous East Coast resort that inspired the game of Monopoly.

One evening in 1930, Darrow sat down and sketched out some of the city's street names on the oilcloth that covered the table. The streets were all from along the Boardwalk, between the Inlet and Park Place, plus Marven Gardens, which he misspelled as Marvin Gardens. He included the three railroads that served the resort and, for symmetry, added the Short Line, which was a freight-carrying bus company with a depot in the city. Houses and hotels were cubes of wood and title deeds for the various properties were typed out on squares of cardboard. The rest of the accessories were easy to get hold of: a pair of dice, some pretend money, and coloured buttons for playing pieces.

From then on, the Darrows' evenings were spent around the kitchen table deep in complex – and imaginary – property deals. Known simply as 'the game', it became a regular pastime for the family and visitors. Friends began to want their own copies of the game. Winners wanted a set so they could show off their financial wizardry; and losers wanted a set to practise so they could avenge their defeat next time. With plenty of free time on his hands, Darrow began making duplicates: soon he was up to two sets a day, and selling them for four dollars each. Through word-of-mouth alone, Darrow soon sold about a hundred sets.

Encouraged by this success, he decided to test the game beyond his circle of friends and acquaintances. He made up more sets and offered them to department stores in nearby Philadelphia. They sold, and the orders kept coming in. His single-handed production line just couldn't keep up and realising his game was marketable, Darrow increased production by

Monopoly. A firm family favourite since the thirties (Hulton Getty)

getting a friend to print the Monopoly boards and title cards. This partial automation enabled him to turn out six games a day, but it still wasn't enough.

By 1934, convinced that his game had huge potential, Darrow arranged to have his friend print and package complete sets. Production was finally keeping pace with demand, but they'd reckoned without Philadelphia's sales season. After one store ordered sets wholesale, in quantities far greater than Darrow and his friend could supply, he was faced with two choices: borrow money and plunge full time into the board-game business, or sell Monopoly to an established games company. He wrote to Parker Brothers, already one of America's major games manufacturers. Parkers were used to enthusiastic inventors sending in new game ideas, and some of them had proven marketable, but they tended to rely on their own staff far more than unproven novices. Monopoly was submitted to their standard assessment routine, with members of staff sitting down in the office to try it out. It proved a winner, but the company had a set of ground rules which had to be satisfied before any game could be successfully marketed. One was that games aimed at families should last no more than forty-five minutes. Monopoly could go on for hours. Also, Parkers believed that every game should also have a specific end, a prize to be won or goal achieved. Monopoly players just kept going round and round the board, the only goal being to bankrupt fellow players and remain solvent. The rules were far too complex. The public would be hopelessly confused trying to learn about mortgages, rents and interest payments.

Ultimately, the game was rejected.

Darrow was furious. He knew that people weren't as dim as Parkers liked to think. Despite their judgement, Monopoly was a marketable commodity and Darrow ordered five thousand sets from his printer friend and continued to sell the game locally. Aware that more Monopoly sets were available, Philadelphia stores placed huge orders for the Christmas season. Darrow found himself working fourteen hours a day just trying to keep up with the packing and dispatching.

Parker Brothers reps soon found out that Philadelphia stores were expecting huge sales of Monopoly and word was passed back to head office. Managers wondered if they should review their earlier decision. After a major New York toystore placed an order for two hundred sets, a friend of the Parker family telephoned to rave about a wonderful new game she had just purchased. The Parker president's daughter and her husband bought a set and ended up playing it at home until the early hours.

The next day, Darrow was invited for a meeting at Parker Brothers' New York office. After insisting on a few revisions and simplification of the rules, Parker Brothers offered to buy the game outright. Darrow would get royalties on all sets sold. Explaining why he had decided to sell, Darrow pointed out the monetary commitment he'd have to have made to keep producing the game himself: 'Taking the precepts of Monopoly to heart,' he said, 'I did not care to speculate.' Royalties from Monopoly soon made Darrow a millionaire. After retiring at forty-six he became a gentleman farmer and a collector of exotic orchids. Years later, commenting on the Parker Brothers offer, he wrote, 'I gladly accepted and have never regretted that decision.'

In 1970, a few years after his death, Atlantic City erected a commemorative plaque in his honour. Unfortunately, despite Lizzie Magie's good intentions, Monopoly's record of inspiring socialism pales into insignificance alongside those who have acquired a definite taste for other people's rent money.

While Charles Darrow was starting to make his millions, on the side of the Atlantic the big news story of 1934 was the 'discovery' of Scotland's Loch Ness Monster. This led to all manner of cash-ins, with a range of toys that centred not so much on the monster's monstrosity as its potential as a soft toy. One of the most popular versions was Sandy the Loch Ness Monster, though there was also an inflatable Monster which could be conveniently fitted in a toy box and came with a catchy song:

I've come from the depths of Loch Ness
My secret I now must confess
As an up to date toy
For a girl or a boy
You will say I'm the latest success.

But not everyone in the 1930s was in such a jolly mood. After a nationwide appeal sponsored by the *Daily Telegraph* and *Morning Post* toys were sent to South Wales to be distributed among the children of the unemployed. The appeal raised £20,000, which bought 180,000 toys (under stipulation that only British-made toys were bought and dispatched). The depression was hitting hard all over Britain and a letter reached the *Morning Post* from the sylvan-sounding but hard-hit Forest of Dean, appealing on behalf of three children – Bill, Jamie and

Susie – orphans who lived in penury with their grandparents. 'Christmas will pass by these waifs unless they can be included in the remit of the press appeal,' said a concerned neighbour, hoping to divert some of the country's charity to their area.

With money so scarce, simple games enjoyed something of a resurgence in the thirties. Chief among these was the jigsaw puzzle. But manufacturers such as Huvanco saw their products as more than simple puzzles: 'These are not cheap daubs or inartistic pictures, but the works of Millais, Raphael, Sargent and Turner, paintings from the Wallace Collection.'

Such defence was likely to excite fresh controversy: was it right that the works of Old Masters be reduced to cheap puzzles for the amusement of the hoi-polloi? This was philistinism of the worst kind. But defenders of the jigsaw puzzle could always pull the heartstrings in their defence if need be. As they were quick to point out, hundreds of thousands of soldiers forgot their wounds and bad memories in the reconstruction of jigsaw pictures. Puzzles were also a solace to the aged and infirm, and an invaluable education to the increasing numbers of children who were beginning to enjoy the pastime.

No doubt these same art snobs would also have objected to toyshop lines such as the Hogarth Crayon and Painting Outfit!

Though the origins of the jigsaw puzzle can be traced back to the dissected maps of the eighteenth century, it wasn't until the early 1900s that they began to be regarded as amusements in their own right. Early puzzles could be quite a challenge, cut as they were along the lines of colour so that visual clues were scarce. Most boxes did not even feature the now-obligatory lid picture to help. Pieces didn't even interlock, so one careless nudge was enough to undo an entire evening's work.

They were quite a challenge to the wallet, too. Since they were cut by hand, one piece at a time, a 500-piece puzzle could cost half a week's wages. No wonder then that it was only high-society folk who could indulge.

But it wasn't long before things got easier. The Parker Brothers' Pastime brand introduced puzzles with familiar objects such as dogs and birds, and interlocking pieces. The

Pastime range of puzzles became so successful that Parker cut back on some of their bestselling games – Rook, Pit, Quit, Tell It to the Judge and Keep off the Grass – and devoted their entire production line to the manufacture of jigsaw puzzles.

On sale in ever-increasing numbers, the puzzles were soon established as a diversion appealing to adults and children alike. With the onset of the Great Depression puzzles for adults reached a peak. In 1933, as a diversion from financial gloom and an inexpensive entertainment, they were selling an amazing ten million a week. Puzzles could be hired from libraries and drugstores for as little as three cents a day.

Mass production and the introduction of die-cut cardboard puzzles meant a substantial further fall in prices. There were even weekly jigsaw puzzles: retailing for twenty-five cents, the Jig of the Week appeared every Wednesday and people clamoured to be the first to complete it. Also appearing were Picture Puzzle Weekly, B-Witching Weekly, Jiggers Weekly and Movie Cut-Ups.

In Britain the jigsaw puzzle was just as popular and many companies embraced it as the perfect promotional toy. The Great Western Railway, for instance, issued a series of scenes from along its main Paddington–Penzance route featuring steam locos like *City of Truro* and coastal scenes of Devon and Cornwall. Available from WH Smith bookstalls on GWR stations, they provided a perfect way for children and their parents to while away a journey which might easily take eight hours or more.

'Are you taking full advantage of the black-out nights?' asked an advert for Waddington's Games. In addition to their games like Shop-Missus, Monopoly and Totopoly, just the ticket for passing a few hours in the Anderson shelter, Waddington's offered a fine range of jigsaws, including such enlightening subjects as the Mappa Mundi, a scrap of medieval cartography that somehow never got mentioned again for nigh on half a century. 'Of particular interest in these stressful days' was a series of Homes and Beauty puzzles, 'a welcome relief from war pictures with calm and peaceful illustrations, beautiful scenes of rural England'.

But not everyone wanted distractions. The war inspired all kinds of exciting toys and games. No sooner was the Battle of the River Plate reported in the press than the toy industry was selling scale models of ships like *Graf Spee*, *Achilles*, *Ajax* and *Exeter* – ready for assembly by an eager and patriotic audience.

The age-old pastime of toy soldiers – beloved by every male from eight to eighty – had updated, if less glamorous, additions. Boys seemed to be just as keen to act out events on the home front. Toyshops had a toy searchlight (twenty-two shillings and sixpence, including an 8-volt battery), an AA gun (forty-two shillings, with a 9-inch barrel and 72 projectiles), and even tin-plate toys like an ARP Decontamination van and an ARP shelter and trench. Tin helmets were especially popular, and there were playsuits based on army and RAF uniforms. Ray's produced Models of the Maginot Line and the Siegfried Line, complete with ammo dumps, trenches, sandbags, pill boxes, AA guns and so on.

Anti-German feelings had left shops with thousands of pounds' worth of unsaleable toys. At the offices of the *Toy Trader* staff were alarmed by a personal visit from one Adolf Hitler. 'Why not in your toyshops any German toys are?' demanded the Führer, brushing past the hapless receptionist to beard the editor at his desk. But no – ho-ho-ho! – it turned out to be one of those jovial toy company reps having a laugh with his firm's latest craze – Hitler masks.

The hated Hitler could be used for sport, too. The Allies Dartboard, for instance, featured Hitler's nose as its bull's-eye and Hang it on Hitler's Nose was a timely reworking of the old hoop-la game, with the Führer's unmistakable conk standing in as a hook.

War shortages – of metals, paper, inks and just about everything else – had put an end to the production of many toys. Fans of construction toys were particularly affected by the squeeze on supplies. Even before the war had kicked off for real, Meccano factories had been setting aside production time to manufacture munitions for the war effort. Now, toy production inevitably sidelined, serious shortages of Meccano parts were inevitable. Complaints were regarded as disloyal, but just so there would be no arguments, in 1943 a government ban was decreed on the sale of any new or second-hand toys made from metal.

Games, being cheaper to produce and having less restriction on materials, were enjoying a mini-boom in popularity. The number of card games in circulation was tremendous. Other cerebral pursuits like stamp-collecting were also enjoying a surge of popularity among young people.

Many of the games had war themes, usually based on beating the enemy, with such victory-inspiring names as Bombs Away! and The Road to Victory. Square one kicks off with the Reichstag fire. From there players have to escape German-occupied territory via France, Italy and Yugoslavia or the Baltic countries. The route to the winning-post is scattered with all kinds of horrible threats to humanity – racial laws, the assassination of Dollfuss and so on. Sunken ships, air-raids, mines and prowling U-boats all add to the family fun. The game ends as the Allies prepare their victory parade and the winner gets to pass sentence on the Nazi Party. There's a choice of three punishments – death, lifelong exile or confinement in a lunatic asylum. 'It's historical! It's instructive! It's a winner!' crowed the adverts. 'And only five shillings and sixpence.' (Little did players realise that they'd have to wait another five years for any of it to become reality.)

Materials may have been in short supply, but there were always ways of obtaining them. In 1943, according to a court case reported in *The Times*, the licensee of the King Henry VIII pub in Hemel Hempstead was given six months in prison for making wooden toys and tanks from aircraft parts stolen from a nearby base. It must have been a large-scale operation, for the materials – plywood, string, rope and paint – were valued at £766. One hopes that the string and plywood were not a vital part of Britain's defences ... if so, perhaps the landlord ought really to have been on a treason charge!

But the world's woes could sometimes provide a sinister example of the swings and roundabouts cliché ... In East Anglia thousands of dolls and other toys were washed ashore from a

Japanese cargo ship that had hit a mine in the North Sea. It was a piece of serendipity which brought great joy to local children. Many of them were evacuees from London, so their luck came with a side dish of poetic justice.

Nazi soldiers could earn themselves two extra days' leave, according to *Hamburger Fremdenblatt*, for the best model aeroplane. As well as alleviating boredom, the exercise was encouraged as a way of teaching troops to recognise enemy aircraft.

A PoW camp visitor from American broadcaster CBS reported that bridge and Monopoly were favourite pastimes among the internees.

With so much of its previously healthy trade ruined by war conditions, toyshops must have been under pressure to diversify. Adverts in the *Toy Trader* suggested that the shops should stock ARP teeth grips. Made of rubber, these blocks were intended for civilians – thousands of them apparently – who couldn't help but clench their teeth during air-raids. The tension was so great that bitten tongues were frequently reported and some hospitals were even called upon to fix broken jaws. It wasn't exactly the joy-bringing stuff that toyshops were used to selling, but they had to make a living somehow.

Children looking forward to sunnier times might have availed themselves of a pair of Palm Beach or Riviera sunglasses, reassuringly 'non-inflammable' and ensuring greater 'eye comfort'. Then again, they might be just as useful for looking at the searchlights as they swept the skies for Luftwaffe bombers.

1945–1960

The immediate post-war years were grim for children in many ways. Sweets and chocolate rationing would continue for another eight years and many were returning from evacuation to bomb-blasted cities. Relief came most usually in the form of sport, and this was the period of all-time record attendances for both cricket and football matches. Never slow to spot a trend, the toy-makers were soon looking to cash in on this sport-mad generation.

Developed in 1947 by Peter Adolph, Subbuteo was a refinement of 'New Footy,' a British table-soccer game introduced in 1920 and later publicly blessed by star players Stanley Matthews and Nat Lofthouse. Common to both games were small figures inserted into flattened semi-spherical bases. These were flicked with the aim of knocking the ball either to another player or, hopefully, into the opposition's goal. Defending goalies had a rod attached to the back of the base, extending through the back of the goal.

New Footy figures were made of lacquered cardboard inserted in a lead base, which made flicking a hard and sometimes painful experience. Another difficulty was that each figure was different and could only be used in its correct position, so the left-winger could only be placed on the left wing, not used as a centre-half.

Peter Adolph's version made use of newly available and lighter plastic for the bases. Printed on to stiff cardboard sheets, Subbuteo figures had to be cut out with scissors and inserted into the base – similar to New Footy ones but more rounded. These figures – known as 'flats' – formed the basic game for twenty years. Their aerodynamic shape allowed them to be

Boy and model railway, 1950-style (Mary Evans Picture Library)

'curled' around opposing players to reach the ball. The goals were made of flat wire with paper netting. No pitch was included, so each set included a piece of chalk for marking out a playing area on a board or an old army blanket, which most homes still had in those days. The biggest advantage of all was that the sets were cheap to produce and cheap to buy, eminent-ly suitable for the hard-pressed post-war period. A company – Subbuteo Sports Games Ltd – was formed to produce and market the new game. It took its name from *falco subbuteo*, the

Latin name for the hobby, a British bird of prey. A stylised image of the bird's head was used for the original Subbuteo crest.

Meanwhile, smaller Meccano sets had been available in the toyshops in time for Christmas 1945; and the parts had reverted to red and green colouring, instead of the austere plain metal used in the few sets on sale during the dark years. But it wasn't all good news: prices had escalated steeply and supplies of steel and brass (both essential metals in Meccano) were still erratic. Nevertheless, by the early fifties *Meccano Magazine* had increased its circulation to 100,000 and in 1952 its sponsored model-building contests featured a working jukebox and a duplicating machine.

In what was no doubt a blow to traditionalists – and Tories – the latest Hornby Dublo trains were issued in the livery of the newly nationalised British Railways. More gritty realism was available courtesy of Airfix's new Railway Trackside series. The first offering was the Country Inn, which one expects wouldn't have been much use to anyone who'd modelled their layout on downtown Wigan.

Railways were still enormously popular and, despite the inexorable decline of steam locomotives, the hobby of trainspotting was in its heyday. The 1960s saw the introduction of Airfix's rolling-stock kits – a tanker wagon and cement wagon, followed by the Diesel Railbus, and various steam locomotives. In an age when trainspotting was the norm and every other boy had an interest in railways, the kits were steady sellers. In 1962 Airfix bought out the renowned Kitmaster company, a firm whose range and attention to detail had made it leader in the market. A limited number of the Kitmaster locos and rolling stock were reintroduced by Airfix, though nothing like the full range that had made Kitmaster products so prized. Though I was really too young truly to appreciate the wonders of the finished product, and it certainly predated my trainspotting years, my mother spent several evenings patiently assembling a Kitmaster model of the *Royal Scot*, carefully lining up the pots of Humbrol paint and dipping in a brush delicately to apply the colours – red for the buffer beam, silver for the buffers and couplings, green for the cab and boiler sections. I watched, puzzled, as my mum fetched a saucer of warm water and soaked the British Railways decals, sliding the loosened transparencies into place on the cabside and tender, gently blowing them dry. After moving the old-fashioned brass ornaments aside, we stood the *Royal Scot* on the windowsill and looked at it, a masterpiece, with its working pistons and coupling rods.

But while the trains could still inspire such adoration, Britons were starting to mutter like never before about railway staff, and their sarcastic jokes soon filtered down to the nation's toyshops. Although the clockwork Mr Porter Luggage Truck was sold without any sly asides, adverts described a similar clockwork figure, the Flying Porter, as 'An amusing novelty porter, running along like mad with his arms full of luggage – unlike real porters these days and reminiscent of the good old days!'

The old order was being challenged in other ways, too. From Denmark, of all places…

Lego, which derived its name from the Danish words *leg godt* – play well – began life in 1949 as Automatic Binding Bricks. Ole Kirk Christiansen, a Danish carpenter, started his Lego company in the 1930s to make and sell a variety of wooden toys. The bricks – initially available only in red and white – had the familiar studs and could be easily stacked. In the early fifties people began to demand a complete system and the bricks were renamed Lego and repackaged with small cars and figures as well as being redesigned to offer even more connecting possibilities. Lego may have been a lot simpler than Meccano, but in the right hands it could offer almost as many constructional challenges, and by the end of the decade it was firmly established as one of the most popular constructional toys in Europe.

Dinky toys were also back in production, but the Meccano firm's supremacy with toy cars, so long without any serious rivals, was under threat…

A couple of years after the end of the war, in June 1947, two unrelated Smiths – Leslie and Rodney, who had served in the Royal Navy together – pooled their resources to buy a second-hand die-casting machine for £750. Calling themselves Lesney Products (from the first half of Leslie and the back end of Rodney) the two Smiths rented a bombed-out pub in north London and started to make electrical components. Business was slow. Desperate for any kind of income from their investment and to fill gaps in their schedule they began to make toys and household items under the tutelage of a third partner, Jack O'Dell, an experienced die-casting designer.

Their first toy was an Aveling Barford road-roller. It was taken on by a few local shops during 1948, but the bigger toyshops were not that keen on stocking the Lesney brand. Word was spreading among toy-starved children, however, and a continual demand for new toys made the retailers change their minds. But just when it looked as if the two Smiths might have found themselves a moneyspinning sideline, bad luck struck. Supplies of metals were restricted during the Korean War, and so Lesney were able to make only one tin-plate toy, Jumbo the Elephant. In 1952, with things returning to normal, they decided to cash in on the forthcoming Coronation with a scale model of the Royal State Coach, complete with figures of Elizabeth and Prince Philip inside. A smaller-scale version, brought out the following year to coincide with the ceremony, produced a pleasant surprise when it sold a million units and gave a welcome boost to Lesney's depleted bank account.

The smaller toys proved to be even more popular and by the end of 1953 the company's range of small-scale toy vehicles comprised a road-roller, cement-mixer, tractor, bulldozer, horse-drawn milk float and a rag and bone cart. When Jack O'Dell's daughter asked if she could take one to school to show her classmates, her dad put it in a small box. However, the box was a one-off and it wasn't until toy buyers at the 1954 Harrogate Toy Fair commented on the lack of attractive packaging that any thought was given to the notion. When the two Smiths relayed the criticisms to O'Dell, he suggested they use the same kind of packaging his daughter had used – 'about the same size and shape as a matchbox'. It solved the packaging problem, and gave the new toys their identity, with a neat and memorable name that would soon become part of every British schoolboy's lingo. Matchbox Toys were born.

The idea of a 'matchbox' to put toys in wasn't exactly original, having been used in Germany as long ago as the early 1900s. And the first Matchbox boxes were hardly attractive, being plain white card with tuck-in ends and no picture. Marketing needed specialised skills and after deciding that their true talents lay in design and manufacture, Lesney contracted the Moko Company to market the toys worldwide. The Matchbox trademark was registered in 1953, with 50 per cent of the rights belonging to Moko and 50 per cent to Lesney. The boxes were redesigned with images of the models, first as drawings, then in more detail, and eventually in colour. In return for Moko's financial input, early boxes carried their brand name alongside Lesney (an arrangement that continued until 1960 when Lesney bought back Moko's 50 per cent interest after the two firms disagreed over plans to expand to the Far East).

Orders to supply some London branches of Woolworth's followed soon after. Lesney had hit the big time. They were still making the larger toys and their Jumbo the Elephant was joined by Muffin the Mule as the firm attempted to ride the TV bandwagon. But it was the smaller Matchbox vehicles that provided their biggest income. Their established range was joined by a red fire-engine and a double-decker London bus, while their 1956 Midget MG gave the firm its biggest boost, opening up the US market.

Almost as soon as Matchbox had hit the big time, they had a rival from just round the corner. In the early 1950s Minimodels, based in Mill Hill, introduced a set of nicely detailed metal cars powered by a novel 'press-down-and-pull-back' keyless clockwork motor. The range – sold under the name of Scalex – featured sports and racing prototypes such as Jaguar, Austin Healey, Aston Martin and Ferrari. Overwinding – the weakness of all clockwork toys – was impossible, according to the sales pitch, at least.

It wasn't until four years later that Fred Francis, the brains behind the Scalex cars, came up with the idea of electric raceway kits. Tabletop racing with miniature cars was already an established hobby in the post-war years, though the tracks in use then had raised rails to guide the cars around the circuit which lacked realism and did not always give satisfactory results. After adapting three of his Scalex models – the Austin-Healey 106, Ferrari 375 F1 and the Maserati 250F – to take an electric motor, Francis devised a special rubber-based track on which to race them. The track's novel feature was the substitution of grooves for rails, with the cars picking up the electric current from beneath the groove by means of a 'gimbal' wheel. The new product was dubbed Scalextric.

After causing a sensation when it was shown at the 1957 Harrogate Toy Fair, the new game even featured on the BBC's *Tonight* programme. With such invaluable free publicity working for it, the firm started full-scale production, with the first Scalextric set costing just under six pounds. Demand soon outstripped the small firm's production capability and Scalex quickly became victims of their own success. Within a year of the launch of the company it was sold wholesale to Tri-ang.

Earlier in the decade the toyshops of Britain had been full to the brim with all manner of novelties designed to cash in on the Coronation fever of 1953, such as the aptly named Longfellow Folding Periscope for those who intended to travel down to London for the event: 'Make sure you see all the Coronation events...' There were souvenir playing cards with backs featuring a radiant Elizabeth, and a topical Crown the Queen card game, invented by Elaine Burton MP. Despite George VI's earlier reluctance to let the Windsor family be exploited, the Palace was learning to play the media game: royal portrait jigsaw puzzles of Elizabeth and her children were to be found in toyshops across the realm. Doubtless a few of her residences appeared in the Famous Castle puzzle series, which also featured hot topical themes such as 'Triumph over Everest'. (Ironically, mountaineer Chris Bonnington was more of a scrabble fan and played that game with his colleagues while ascending Annapurna.)

In 1954 Britain's new Queen attended the British Industries Fair. Toy manufacture was acknowledged as a vital part of the national economy and the various toy company stands certainly offered more amusement (and newspaper copy) than ones which tried to interest visitors in paperclip-bending devices and plastic button-making machines. The royal couple both laughed at the puppets on show, but Her Majesty declined an invitation to insert her regal hand in one, saying, 'It looks too complicated.' This was either a remarkable indictment of the Windsor family IQ or else its snobbery about contact with the hoi-polloi.

Perhaps it was the word put out on the puppet grapevine that inspired the disgraceful display of anarchy at the Chad Valley stand, where HM was accosted by Harry Corbett and Sooty. The yellow bear pointed his water pistol at the royals and a thin stream of water fell on the Duke's jacket, while the Queen herself managed to dodge a soaking. It was described as 'an amusing episode' by the deferential hacks of the day.

The Duke appeared puzzled by Mr Potato Head, until the Queen explained the principles and the couple spent an amusing few minutes looking it over. Little did anyone suspect that fifty years on this spud of many faces would enjoy Hollywood status as a co-star in *Toy Story*. Mr Potato Head – 'the most wonderful friend a boy and girl could have' – but not for long if their dad owned a chip shop – was devised in 1950 when American George Lerner, inspired by his children playing with their food, decided to turn the bad habit into a toy. After unsuccessfully looking for a major backer, Lerner sold the idea for a piddling $500 to a breakfast food company who planned to give the pieces away in boxes of cornflakes. It might not have seemed like a bad pay-off, but it could have cost Lerner millions. A further meeting with Hasbro brought immediate interest in Mr Potato Head and they were keen enough to make Lerner an offer – but Lerner no longer owned the rights! Hasbro were so determined to own Mr Potato Head they paid the cereal company $2,000 to stop production and return the rights.

Mr Potato Head had a wife, and a son and daughter, Spud and Yam. But this all-American family set-up had some bad habits. In 1987, under pressure from America's health lobby, the hapless papa spud was forced to give up his pipe (as if children were going to use him as a role-model anyway!). The PC bullies made a big deal of it and the pipe was cere-monially handed over to America's Surgeon-General at a press conference.

Back in the 1950s rubber was making its mark, both for its versatility and its harmlessness. All kinds of lethal weapons could be wielded and rubber made it all a cartoon-style joke. Marklin made model cannons that fired rubber shells, while those who preferred a hands-on approach could wield a rubber policeman's truncheon or even a caveman's club. Its uses for practical jokers were legion. 'The average Briton makes an excellent subject. His sense of humour is more highly devel-oped,' touted one jingoistic ad. Rubber was the ideal medium and it came in many forms – joke fruit, joke fried eggs, joke biscuits, joke sweets – not forgetting the wobbly pencil which was, according to the *Daily Mail*, 'the joke purchased by the Queen at the British Industries Festival' – though one can't imagine her repeating the accompanying slogan: 'Will it write? Will it ...!'

Rubber, then, was the source of plenty of fun, and one manufacturer that aimed primarily at more grown-up enter-tainment, the London Rubber Company, also made 100 million balloons each year.

Before moving on from the toys area, the Queen bought Slinky – the walking spring. 'How amusing,' she said. 'I'll have one of those' (dialogue courtesy of the *Daily Mail*). Oddly enough, the prototype Slinky was conceived not as a toy but as an anti-vibration device for naval instruments. Lacking success in that area, its inventor Richard James went on to win busi-ness by remarketing it as a toy. The Queen also picked up a clacking space gun. According to the *Evening News*, 'the famous royal smile lit her face as she pointed the gun at the ceiling and listened to its sinister purr.'

In spite of the Queen's Scottish parentage (on the non-German side, at least), it is unclear whether the Matchbox Coronation Coach was sold in toyshops north of the border. It may not have gone down at all well if it had. Bricks had already been thrown through the windows of some Scottish shops that had displays celebrating the forthcoming Coronation of (the so-called) Elizabeth the Second. True Scots, if they deigned to recognise the new queen at all, would only regard her as Elizabeth the First. Scottish retailers, far from being angry at their glaziers' bill, were inclined to be stoical and took the broken windows as a warning. 'The wise seller does not offend even a small section of his customers,' said one correspondent to the *Toy Trade Journal*. A rich statement, considering some of the items on sale in toyshops, which included something likely to offend nearly every minority section of the population. Quite apart from Scottish string puppet Scotty McBoozle – 'the red-nosed Glaswegian drunk!' – there were all manner of other dubious items. The first wave of West Indian immigration had done little to change ingrained British views of black people and they were more often as not cast as clowns and fools – as exemplified by the Coloured Coon Windmill, which boasted moving eyes and tongue. Much of the fascination seemed to revolve around African dancing and music: Jiggling Jimmy – 'I'm the rage, I'm the craze' – was a mechanical high-steppin' tap dancer. Described as 'a gaily coloured nigger minstrel on a metal base', Jiggling Jimmy was made to dance by means of a fingered lever. Musical Dandies, also black, were figures attached to the top of a mouth organ. While blowing into the harmonica, the player manipulated a lever to make the dandies dance. Patronising certainly, and possibly inspired by movies including scenes of the local sheriff demanding a jig with a few casually aimed bullets!

If racism was all-pervasive, sexism wasn't far behind. Female figures were cast in a variety of stereotyped roles: from Ma'mselle Fi-fi ('your daintiest gold-digger for the season, the blonde they all prefer'), to Rosebud's Hula Girls (saucy bathing belles wearing brief bikini swimsuits), Walk Talk Dolls ('with

Six-year-old Richard Lane from Norwich, 'wearing an interplanetary space helmet' takes a ride in a Dan Dare spaceship at the 1954 British Industries Fair, Earl's Court, London (Hulton Getty)

flirting eyes') and Pedigree Perfect Dolls ('with roving eyes that really flirt outrageously'). And while the dolls were all rolling eyes and flirtation, the (male) factory bosses ensured that their real-life employees made the best of themselves: one Glasgow factory gave its girls compulsory manicures (ten minutes for each girl every ten days). The firm also offered chiropody, but this was voluntary. If they were lucky, these girls may well have sported Steady Rings on their beautifully manicured fingers: the rings for girls who wanted 'to belong'.

Toys could be put to many uses. At an Ipswich house, they

were used to lure a poltergeist out of hiding for an exorcism – which seems rather a mean trick! Ghostbuster in chief, one Mr Sharp of the local Spiritualist Church, was of the opinion that they were dealing with the spirit of a young person who'd been deprived of material things in his earthly life. This theory seemed to be confirmed when Sharp went into a trance. 'I am drowning,' wailed the spirit voice. 'I was drowned ten years ago. I never had anything for Christmas.' This clairaudience was followed shortly afterwards by a series of odd events: a key was lifted from its hook, Christmas decorations were torn from the wall, coathangers were rattled in the wardrobe, and a book with the title *Keep off My Ranch* was thrown across the living room, narrowly missing Sharp. Which all goes to show that even on the other side, where toys are concerned, temper tantrums are never too far behind.

After investigating local newspaper archives Sharp came up with the theory that the spirit probably belonged to a local boy who had drowned in a nearby millstream. He suggested leaving toys at the spot, which the householders did.

It wasn't only the poor drowned lad who was the recipient of free toys. In the post-war years the deprivation of a genera-tion led the kindly sounding Miss Dorothy Knill to announce (in a letter to *The Times*, no less) the formation of the Yellow Duck Club to provide toys to the needy.

But if things were bad in Britain, obviously they were much worse in the routed Germany. 'MOTHERS OF NUREMBERG PROTEST AGAINST WAR TOYS.' So read one of the placards of the women who gathered to picket a toy-trade exhibition there. Some of the other placards had a list of guilty firms attached. The local police moved the mothers on, but they were allowed to return once the names had been crossed out.

Despite these noble efforts, the Second World War was still fresh in the memories of children and more a cause of excite-ment than despair. Indeed, it was almost like a must-have brand for many of the toys produced in the years immediately after-wards. Even the most innocuous items acquired a war dimen-sion – like the pencil box (with built-in sharpener) fashioned into the shape of an aircraft carrier. Soldiers and toy guns had been around for generations – and would no doubt continue to be so for as long as there were wars – but children wanted to be up to date, too. The onset of the Cold War had children acting out their own Berlin Airlift games with remote-controlled helicopters, injured airmen, dropping provisions or Red Cross supplies.

In the fifties nobody seemed concerned that children were playing with toy soldiers; it was what the soldiers were made out of that was a worry. The use of lead was beginning to concern some people, and the popularisation of plastic was welcomed by wary parents. In 1951 M. Zang and R. Selwyn-Smith formed a company to make 54mm plastic figures of modern troops and 'traditional Westerners'. The Herald trademark was adopted in 1953 and a couple of years later the firm became an associate company of Britains, leading to rapid expansion. The Swoppets range featured British infantry of the Second World War, figures from the English and American civil wars, Highlanders, Trojans, a Robin Hood set and even a group of polar explorers. The best set, according to collectors, was the Wars of the Roses, whose figures displayed an incredible devotion to the minutest detail of the weapons.

Toy soldiers remained popular into the 1960s and the Miniature Figures series, marketed by Airfix in boxed sets of forty, covered a huge range of military and civilian subjects. Alongside the good guys and bad guys from the two World Wars – Italian, Japanese, German, British, French and American troops – there were figures from both sides of the American Civil War and the Battle of Waterloo. Other sets of opposing forces featured Romans and ancient Britons, Cowboys and Indians, and Robin Hood and the Sheriff of Nottingham. The series was eclectic enough to embrace subjects as diverse as Arabs and Astronauts. With the growing influence of TV, Airfix even issued a set based on the BBC2 Western programme *High Chaparral*.

Airfix was just about the biggest name in toys and models by the 1950s. Founded in 1939 by Nicholas Kove, a Hungarian

Jew, the original business, based in London, was set up to make cheap rubber toys filled with air – hence the name, Airfix. After investing in one of the first injection-moulding machines in Britain, the firm diversified into making plastic pocket combs. They quickly became the largest comb-makers in the country, though directors managed to resist the temptation to change the firm's name to Hairfix!

Commissioned to produce a promotional toy tractor but saddled with a budget that would not stretch to making assembled examples, Airfix resolved the problem by producing the toy in D-I-Y kit form. This model – selling at two shillings and elevenpence – was their very first venture into the field. Having glimpsed the commercial possibilities, the firm followed up by devising their first proper Airfix kit – Sir Francis Drake's ship *Golden Hind*. The prototype was pitched to Woolworth's toy buyers, who liked it but insisted they could not sell if for more than two shillings – half the price proposed by Airfix. Realising that too much of their costs were going on attractively designed boxes, a compromise was reached and the kit appeared in the shops packaged in a clear plastic bag sealed with a simple header card. It was a sound move. After years of austerity, the post-war population was too interested in the new toy's novelty to be put off by the plain packaging and the *Golden Hind* model proved to be an enormous success.

In 1953 Airfix released the first of its aircraft models – the Spitfire Mk I, but it wasn't until 1962 that one of the greatest advances in model-making took place with the advent of the 'exploded diagram'. Until then most model-building instructions had been written out in a numbered step-by-step fashion. The exploded diagram meant redundancy notices for the copy-writers and translators who'd translated the instructions into languages as diverse as Hungarian, Danish and Afrikaans.

Anyone who wanted to stop boys' fascination with all things military certainly had their work cut out. From buccaneers' pistols to special agents' revolvers to Dan Dare's Atomic Jet Gun, it was every boy's right to bear firearms. The pages of trade journals were packed with guns: one advert alone offered the Cisco

Kid, Cub, Captain Cutlass, Rip McCoy, à Canadian Mountie gun and holster, Dick Turpin pistol, Dan Dare's Sonic Beam Gun, Winchester, Lone Star, Sharpshooter and Peacemaker – all guaranteed to yield 'bull's-eye profits'.

Hopalong Cassidy merchandising was to the fore and 'America's favourite Western star' arrived at London's Heathrow Airport with forty-eight American boys (one from each state). The intention was to team up with forty-eight British boys and go off on a fourteen-day friendship tour of the UK, staying in Butlin's holiday camps at Clacton, Filey, Skegness, Ayr and Pwllheli. For just over two pounds parents could buy their offspring a cowboy suit and a real blocked felt hat. Some suits were even reversible: a gun-totin' cowboy could duck down behind the wall, do a quick change, and come out as a cheerful Cherokee – quite a useful dodge when things were looking risky.

There were guns and rifles and hats and holster sets galore, but childhood hadn't been totally taken over by the Wild West. If Cowboys and Indians was wildly popular, sci-fi ran it a close second. 'Space toys, atomic guns, carpet sweepers and steam irons have ousted toy soldiers, trains and tea-sets from the nursery,' lamented one industry observer. The Lone Star Ultra Sonic Beam Gun boasted thirteen features, including high-frequency electron buzzer, thorium filament chamber, plutonium power chamber, built-in Geiger counter on the handle, and red, white and green flashes.

The range of playsuits revealed an eclectic choice of role-models, from Robin Hood to Dan Dare, with just about every other career choice along the way: cowgirl, Kentucky boy, Red Indian, nurse, Roy Rogers, Jet Morgan, Speedway ace, pirate. The Big Game Hunter set featured a plastic pith helmet and water pistol.

The unifying feature of virtually all of these, of course, was that no matter if he was playing a pirate or a sci-fi hero, the boy had a gun in his hand. There was Selco, the all-plastic revolver; the Click, 'with convincing sound' (of an empty magazine?); Flash, battery-operated with flashing light when the trigger was pressed; and the quaintly named Puff, which discharged a cloud of fine powder to simulate gunsmoke. Caps – properly known as amorces and sold in tiny round boxes for one penny – held a peculiar fascination for young boys. Quite apart from the bangs and flashes they gave to playing Cowboys and Indians, they could be used in all kinds of unofficial ways. Older boys would lay out a strip on a smooth paving slab and flick the side of a coin all the way along it, setting off an arpeggio of bangs, filling nostrils with the acrid whiff of gunpowder. More foolhardy kids performed a similar trick with their thumbnails – a risky display of bravado which many failed to get the hang of, judging by their discoloured digits. Or you could make a mini-bonfire with a few sweet wrappers and lollipop sticks and chuck the whole box of caps on to it. It's probable that these were the same nutters who went on to empty the gunpowder out of fireworks and made a pile on to which they dropped a match. For the full derring-do effect it was necessary to move back with perfect timing (an acquaintance of mine who wasn't quick enough spent the next three months growing back his eyebrows).

Guns were always far more fun with some kind of ammunition. Those who were too young for a Big Chief Airgun could find plenty of alternatives, though some were only marginally less painful. The Telex Repeater Pistol fired wooden slugs up to twenty feet; the Elastoc Pistol fired elastic bands; the Papermatic, as its name implied, simply fired folded nibs of paper. Mums who found their potato supplies mysteriously dwindling could usually trace the reason to something like the Spud Potato Gun. Slightly less harmful, though just as annoying, was the ubiquitous water pistol, of which there were many varieties. The Jetfire – 'the gun sensation of the century' – fired water while simultaneously setting off a cap. With the Texan Sheriff 'One fill gives 1,000 shots,' boasted the adverts, a claim which is somewhat hard to believe.

Children's imaginations ranged across the centuries, from the Silver Knight set with its twelve-inch shield and seventeen-inch plastic sword – 'topically timed to coincide with a spate of romantic chivalry films' – to a plethora of space-age toys. The Dan Dare Space Ship 'launches to 150 feet and returns to earth with help of nylon parachute, while for those who not only wanted to blast the baddies with their ray-gun but wanted to communicate the fact back down to earth there were the Space Ace Phone and the Dan Dare Tele-Electric Space Helmet ('includes Morse Code key!'). Pirates were popular, too, partially due to the TV appearances of Captain Pugwash, and toyshops could do you a Swashbuckling Pirate's sword with cut-out hat and paper eye-patch, or the plastic Pirate Raft – 'sails in the Bathtub Sea' – complete with treasure chest, skull and crossbones flag and grog barrel.

Away from the high seas, real-life piracy was already a bone of contention in the toy trade. Offended businessmen often turned to a bit of well-aimed racism to decry the practice, as when a Hong Kong manufacturer started to export copies of British-made dolls to Britain: 'The infernal sauce of some of these Asiatic gentlemen,' ranted one editorial in the *Toy Trade Journal*. But such competition was virtually impossible to stop, especially once the toys were on the shelves. Imports could only be blocked by use of an injunction that would allow them to be impounded on arrival.

The British toy industry was not without its own wily practices. To protect their profits established companies were quite capable of stabbing newcomers in the back if it helped to eliminate competition, as one well-known New Zealand academic recalls about his mother's modest Teddy bear business. 'It happened at a time when my father was unemployed and my mother made a small Teddy bear. Unknown to her, my father took the bear along to Bournemouth's biggest department store, Beales. After some difficulty he managed to get an audience with the shop's toy buyer. The man took one look and, after discussing a price, he ordered four dozen of the Teddy bears, to be delivered a.s.a.p. My father rushed home to tell my mother the news. After getting hold of two sewing-machines, she recruited some help from a couple of neighbours and together they made the forty-eight bears. More orders followed and my father was soon touring the south of England taking samples to other stores. Things were looking bright. After stripping out the top floor of our house, a production line was set up and we called ourselves "Marjorie Lawrence Soft Toys".

'Over the next couple of years we expanded through the southern counties and had about six employees. But our success was beginning to rattle some of the established toy firms. At the height of production our biggest rival – Tansad – exerted pressure and managed to cut off our supplies of cloth, stuffing and glass eyes. Without materials we went out of business within a few days!

'In those days there was little legal protection against this unethical suppression of competition. I remember as a child seeing bears all around the house, some wearing little overalls, sitting in rows waiting for their eyes to be put in, and begging my mother to put them in so they could see. My mother had a basic pattern, but as there was no absolute standard every one of our bears had a different expression. That was half their charm.'

Although 'hard-nosed toy firm managing director' was probably not a role that appealed to the child of the fifties, virtually every adult activity or occupation was available in a scaled-down version in the toyshops. In the days before the teenager was invented and grew to be a self-important monster, children appear much more willing to be a happy little helper, a carbon-copy good citizen concerned with nothing more than housework or gardening. Such role-playing also continued well into the teens, in contrast to today whereas children want to (or are forced to) become fully fledged consumers at an ever-earlier age.

'Toy of the Century' – something of a bold claim as it was only the early 1950s when the advert appeared – was the Ever Ready Dustette toy vacuum-cleaner. Meanwhile, 'Every little girl will want a Vulcan Washing Machine. She can fill it with water and soapflakes and put in her doll's clothes. When they're clean she simply puts them through the wringer – just like Mummy does!' And once through the wringer, obviously the young misses needed a model iron and ironing board, and a clothes horse – all must-have toys. Toy irons were often described as 'just like Mummy's', but the demand put people at risk from rogue traders. One imported toy iron had a life-sized two-pin plug that neatly fitted into live electrical sockets! The Board of Trade was so alarmed that warnings were circulated to all toyshops and manufacturers were advised to make sure that toy household appliances could never be connected to the mains. And the Ministry of Health felt obliged to issue parents with warnings about buying their children toy pills, presumably to help them recover from their play electrocution.

To go with their white goods girls (or their parents) could buy miniature packets and tins of Hartley's jelly, Bisto, Sifta salt and Pearce Duff's custard powder. Once they'd done the washing and ironing and cooked the dinner the junior house-wives could relax in front of their Kiddies Television or listen to four-inch records on their Gram-O-Fun.

Boys were just as keen to slip into their allotted roles, whether it involved getting behind the handlebars of the Remanco toy lawnmower or the steering-wheel of the Junior Driver set. One of the most exciting products – for boys at any rate – was the Tonka Dump Truck. These sturdy American trucks were what boys had been wishing for all these years. Massively bigger than Dinky toys, the all-steel Tonka trucks had satisfyingly solid tyres and were strong enough to carry a (somewhat peculiar, admittedly) grown man. The toys took their name from Lake Minnetonka near Minneapolis, where the manufacturer had its first base in an old school building at the lakeside. Originally known as Mound Metalcraft, the firm started out making metal display racks and garden utensils, and it wasn't until 1946 that they acquired the machinery necessary to make toys, their first models being a steam shovel and a crane. In the first year the six-strong workforce turned out 37,000 of them, to be greeted with rapture by a post-war generation looking for new toys with style and quality.

When Britain's little girls had done enough role-playing to move on to real-life motherhood, Tri-ang was ready and

Wash day for baby, circa 1945 (Hulton Getty)

waiting with all the equipment. The firm's Pedigree prams were *de rigueur* and the company's Travelling Pram Show was an annual event that visited all the major towns such as Birmingham, Glasgow, Bristol, Cardiff, Newcastle and Nottingham. Just in case any of the new mothers were unsure of their charges, they could always buy a set of Green Monk jingle clips for bike or pram – 'gives instant warning of approach to pedestrians'.

The firm now had its own magazine, *Tri-ang News*, featuring a cover girl: 1955's was twenty-five-year-old Patricia Leicester (the two runners-up were also named Patricia!), selected by Jimmy Hanley, the fresh-faced rookie policeman in the film *The Blue Lamp*. During the war Tri-ang's parent company, Lines, had devoted its energies to munitions work and the 7,000 employees turned out 1 million Sten guns, 11 million magazines, 14 million land-mines, 4,500 gliders, and billions of bullets, shells and fuses. Patriotically, the firm made no charge for improvements to their products, a policy that saved the government millions of pounds when the Mark II Sten gun was adopted by the British Army.

One of Tri-ang's biggest rivals, at least in the junior mobility market, was Mobo, a familiar brand to children of the fifties and sixties. The firm was a pioneer in self-promotion: Mo and Bo were the company's two mascots and fans of Saturday-morning cinema were treated to a Mobo promotional film – *Her Dream Came True* – featuring child stars Yvonne Prestridge and Jonnie Maguire.

The toys produced by Mobo were marketed relentlessly: 'The Mobo rocking horse is a *real* horse – which will appeal to children of today who like realism in their playthings' was stretching it somewhat as the Mobo rocking-horse was no more *real* than any of its numerous forebears. At least children really could 'trundle through the tulips on a snail in spring' if their parents bought them the Mobo Snail. Advertised as 'a fine pal for kiddies from 2–6' and priced at fifty-four shillings and ninepence, the ride-along Mobo Snail was all the rage and made a guest appearance in the *Puss-in-Boots* panto at the London Palladium. From the same bizarre menagerie of tin-plated ride-along toys came the Mobo Toy-toise, and the Mobo Puppy – a spaniel to join the established Mobo Scottie – which 'has the same mechanism and the same gay kennel'. One member of the Mobo zoo even played a sneaky part in the court appearance of two amateur playwrights – Rex Deering and George Young – who were fined ten pounds each by Salford magistrates for using a pantomime script not licensed by the Lord Chamberlain. The script had been approved in 1937, but topical references to power cuts and the Mobo Bronco were taken as proof that the writers had made illicit additions to the dialogue.

All kinds of liberties were taken with the animal kingdom and any child who went on to a career in zoology was due for a nasty shock. There was the Sparking Crocodile, which as the name suggests emitted sparks as it crawled along, and a plastic duck which boasted some distinctly un-duck-like behaviour: 'I roll my eyes, jabber away and run around.' Tri-ang produced a series of clockwork beasts that included the Loch Ness Monster, a Jabberwocky, a mouse with 'special mechanism to give realistic zig-zag movements as it crosses the floor' and a spider with only four legs that was obviously not intended as an educational aid! The only vaguely trustworthy animal toy, it seems, was the Walking Dog, with its 'reliable clockwork actions', though Oliver and Greedy Fish floating bath toy also had a modicum of realism: 'Pop a pellet in his mouth and he goes to the bottom, then pops up for more!'

One great fan of angling, the Queen Mother, might have been entertained, but, along with Chris Bonnington, her favourite game was Scrabble, at least according to newspaper reports of her 1954 visit to New York. Richard Nixon similarly claimed it was his preferred form of relaxation.

'If there hadn't been a Depression in the Thirties there wouldn't have been any Scrabble,' said Alfred Butts, the game's inventor. That's debatable as the idea wasn't entirely new. Lewis Carroll mused in his 1880 diary: 'A game might be made of letters, to be moved about on a chess-board till they form words,' and in 1895 he wrote of a game of his own invention which sounded remarkably similar to Scrabble, with players drawing their letters from a bag.

As an unemployed New York architect, Butts whiled away his jobless days with a word game he'd devised using letters printed on small cardboard squares, combining features of anagrams and crossword puzzles. Careful study of the *New York Times* helped him decide on letter distribution and frequency. The game was originally played without a board, but Butts soon realised that this was an error. He also had doubts about the name he'd come up with – Lexiko – and changed it to It and then Criss-Cross.

A few Criss-Cross sets were made to sell to Butts' friends and neighbours, but established game manufacturers were unanimous in rejecting the game. Then Butts met James Brunot, a game-loving entrepreneur who was rather more enthusiastic about the potential. Together, the two men refined the rules and design and decided on a new name – Scrabble – which they trademarked in 1948. Brunot and his wife rented an old schoolhouse in Dodgington, Connecticut, and began to turn out the games by hand, stamping letters on wooden tiles one at a time. The first years were a struggle. In 1949 the Brunots made 2,400 sets, and a net loss of $450. Sales remained sluggish until 1952 when the owner of Macy's department store chanced to play the game while on vacation and instructed the toy department to stock it. Other toyshops followed suit and the game's reputation was assured. So quickly did the Scrabble craze spread that Chad Valley were forced to discontinue their existing game of Scramble because of confusion with the far more successful Scrabble.

A standard set originally cost three dollars but a de-luxe version with white plastic tiles was available for ten. Plastic tiles eventually became the norm, apparently because sharp-eyed players were able to memorise the grain in the wood to help them pick the letters they needed!

Today there are versions of the game in many languages, each with its particular set of letters. The French version has fifteen 'E's, and since 'Q' is not worth much due to its frequency, 'W' is their most valuable letter. The Spanish set includes tiles for 'CH', 'LL' and 'RR', while the German game has 'Ä', 'Ö' and 'Ü'. An expert player could probably tell you immediately how much 'umlaut' would score! Scrabble nuts maintain that it's possible to score more than 4,000 points in a single game, by using such everyday words as benzoxycamphors, diazohydroxides and oxyphenbutazone.

Another perennial favourite, Cluedo, was devised by Anthony Pratt, a Birmingham solicitor's clerk, in 1949. Unlike many game devisers, Pratt didn't have a drawn-out struggle for acceptance: the game was taken on quite readily by the Leeds firm of Waddington's and proved their judgement right when it became a global success. The name was a simple play on the word Ludo, though it had to be changed to the more literal

Clue for the US market. The pun wouldn't have worked there, because what the British know as Ludo is known as Parcheesi on the other side of the Atlantic. Pratt's original version of the game contained such weapons as a bomb and a hypodermic syringe. No motive for the murder of Doctor Black has ever been put forward.

There are many foreign versions of the game, some of which exert a peculiar fascination. Other nations have turned Colonel Mustard into Madam Curry, Miss Scarlet into Fraulein Ming and Mrs Peacock into Baroness von Blau. Yet, apart from their names, the Cluedo characters were for a long time rather colourless. It wasn't until the 1980s that they acquired fore-names – Dr Claud Black, Colonel Frank Mustard, Mrs Evadne Peacock, Professor Edgar Plum and Miss Flora Scarlett. Despite being the only one with professional access to a font, the Reverend Green was left out of this, though a Cluedo players' handbook has him listed as the Reverend Horatio Green. This same book also lets drop the fact that Mrs Peacock and Professor Plum are siblings.

When girls of the fifties got bored with bumping off their own siblings with an iron bar, the likelihood was that they'd go back to their dolls. As far as many in the toy trade were concerned, British manufacturers still failed to come up to scratch where dolls were concerned. Although he had 'lost ten years to Adolf Hitler and his thugs' and had every reason to loathe the Germans, one toyshop owner felt obliged to give credit to the erstwhile enemy. 'We British may be good plodders, but we can't make mechanical toys – and certainly not dolls. Our doll manufacturers have never seen a real baby or it is certain they would not turn out the shocking specimens we are offered today. As for Italian dolls, they are really works of art and always sell despite high prices.'

The foreign dolls, however, weren't always as perfect as their devotees made out. Looks weren't everything – what was on the inside counted just as much if not more. People had been alerted to the dangers of dirty stuffing. Some manufacturers would use any old unwashed rags so long as they were cheap, but this was risky for the tots who liked to suck their favourite Teddies. The British government passed a new law – the Rag Flock Act of 1951 – to make sure that all soft toys posed no risk to children. Imports especially should be tested for hygiene standards.

Anyway, perhaps British children didn't have time for works of art, hygienic or not. They wanted novelty and noise, like the Singing and Talking Doll, whose name rather sold it short as it 'sings, talks, cries, laughs and gurgles. With an ingenious soundtrack inside which produces a real human voice' or the Cry Baby Doll ('Pinch his lolly and he wails – give it back and he laughs – the greatest noise toy ever!'). There was even a Swimming Doll ('rustproof, clockwork, for bath or pond, swims up to 25 yards!').

Puppets and dummies were also popular. One of the biggest sellers in the fifties was the Archie Andrews Ventro Doll, based on the famous star of theatre and radio. For children on a budget, there was the Archie Andrews Mascot, with full instructions on 'how to be a ventriloquist'. The mascot was just Archie's head on a chrome chain, but 'his eyes roll! his lips move!'. It was good enough to practise with. Marionettes were a favourite plaything and shops had an amazing roll-call: a princess, Chinaman, policeman, clown, minstrel, a spiv, barrow boy, Cossack, parson, cowboy and country squire. All were available separately and were perhaps best dealt with like that. After all, it would surely take a theatrical genius to pen a play involving such a motley cast!

For those looking to create their own characters, there wasn't long to wait. The perfect medium for budding caricature-makers and prototype designers would soon be making its way across the Atlantic. There seems to be a tradition of soap-sellers finding accidental fortunes in unrelated fields. Just as William Wrigley Jr made his millions by exchanging the sadness of soap for the glamour of gum, the inventor of Play-Doh also worked for his father's cleaning-products firm. Joe McVicker's great escape from a life of detergent drudgery came when his sister-in-law, a teacher, grumbled about the modelling clay at her school being too hard for little fingers to manipulate. Joe thought he had the answer: a putty-like substance which he'd formulated to clean wallpaper, but which was soft, malleable and – crucially – stayed that way as long as it was kept in an airtight container. After a few tests to make sure it was safe – i.e., that any tots who chose to eat it wouldn't drop dead – he sent a sample to the school. After receiving the thumbs-up from his sister-in-law and her class, his first contract came from the Cincinnati Board of Education, who agreed to buy it for all the kindergartens and schools in their area. The child-friendly stuff was showcased at an educational convention and by 1956 the D-I-Y product-turned-kids'-toy had become 'Play-Doh', the original reusable modelling compound. Returned to its tub after use (oh, the optimism of toy-makers!), Play-Doh could be used again and again – 'for endless fun', as the toy business was wont to say. As everyone knows, when left out for more than a day or so, the stuff sets hard as a rock.

Play-Doh became such a steady seller that the family business soon changed its name from boring Kutol Chemicals to the more cuddly Rainbow Crafts, despite the fact that Play-Doh was available only in dull white until the company chemist decided to broaden its appeal by adding colours, and the now-familiar smell. As for Joe, he was a millionaire by the age of twenty-seven, having made plenty of dough from his Play-Doh.

While Play-Doh has proved to be an enduring favourite, crazes came and went with predictable regularity. In 1947 Hansburg remodelled the old favourite the pogo stick. Called the Master Pogo, it had a longer-lasting spring and for a while ruled supreme on the streets of America. Among the fifties fads, most now long forgotten, was the Revojet, a cross between a kite and an aeroplane. Bank holidays at Blackpool were full of them: they consisted of a twin circular track on a handle and a two-inch ball which the player had to keep revolving by centrifugal force. The Boogie Woogie Bird – 'walks up walls, walks on ceilings!' – was quickly surpassed by another craze, the Doodler – a mobile wire framework around which one had to manoeuvre a metal ring on the end of a stick without it touching. 'It will make you the life of the party,' said the adverts, adding far-fetched claims for it as a smoking cure and a remedy for neurotics. The *Daily Express* even made a doughty attempt to revive the yo-yo.

But the one that stayed longest in people's memories was the hula hoop, a craze which gripped Britain and America in the final years of the decade. Though it had its origins way back in the ancient world (and was named by eighteenth-century missionaries who saw it being gyrated around the tummies of Hawaiian lovelies), the hula hoop was relaunched by the gloriously titled Wham-O Manufacturing Inc. (which sounds rather like one of those firms beloved of Dennis the Menace whose sole *raison d'être* was the production of stink bombs and itching powder). Made out of cheap plastic and costing under two dollars, the hula hoop soon notched up worldwide sales of 100 million and the shareholders of Wham-O were soon laughing all the way to the bank.

Though wildly popular in the West, the hula hoop was greeted with disdain in Eastern Europe where hardline Marxists cited it as yet another example of the emptiness of American culture.

Twenty-first-century children may be puzzled by the hula hoop's popularity but there were plenty of other toys around in the fifties that would be greeted with equal bemusement today. For instance, magnetic toys featured prominently in toyshops of the fifties. Magnetic Joan and Magnetic Molly were two-dimensional dolls, each of which came with a set of magnetic clothes which girls could mix and match – a cleverer version of the weekly paper 'n' scissors feature that appeared in the girls' comic *Bunty*. Boys were not forgotten and their version – Up Guards! – featured a magnetic ten-inch soldier with eight attachable uniforms. Toreador and bull were another magnetic novelty, featuring two figures that swivelled towards each other as if in combat. With Moody the Mule all you needed to do was 'show him the special turnip and Moody awakes. His mouth opens and his head will follow each move of the vegetable. A magnetic sensation!' There was also a set of Magnetic Dogs – 'you just can't keep them away from each other!' – though it's unclear which ends of the dogs had the magnetic attraction...

Perhaps the most popular magnetic toy was Woolly Willy, a down-in-the-mouth bald chap. The plastic-covered portrait came with a mound of iron filings and your job was to bring some dignity back to him by using the magnetic wand to arrange these on his pate, chin and upper lip. His hairstyle was completely in your power!

More familiar to parents of today is the use of merchandising tie-ins that started to be fully explored in the fifties. 'One might be tempted to predict a TV Christmas,' *Toy Trade Journal* prophesied in 1955. Four years earlier Hulton enterprises had already received their first wodge of royalties from *Eagle/Swift/Girl* and *Robin* comic merchandising – mainly due to the millions of fans who listened to the weekly *Dan Dare* episodes on Radio Luxembourg: 'Devoid of bulging muscles, cloaks of invisibility and magical powers, Colonel Dare tackles his problems with the same discipline and resourcefulness common to the best service traditions!' The shops were full of Dan Dare paraphernalia, plus puppets based on *Eagle* stalwarts like Harris Tweed and Lettice Leafe.

TV's influence was increasingly reflected on the shelves of Britain's toyshops and in 1954 the Sooty Xylophone was the year's bestselling toy. Though long since copyrighted to the Corbetts – father Harry and son Matthew – the original Sooty was just a nameless Chad Valley glove puppet that Harry picked up in a seaside gift shop. The electrician and part-time magician thought it would be the ideal companion to amuse junior audiences and fortune smiled on the duo. After Harry and Sooty won a talent contest in 1952 the BBC offered them

While Dan Dare spin-offs represented space mania in British and American toy-making in the fifties, the Germans were busy developing their own remote-controlled rocket (right), which, after being launched, 'shot to a height of 28 yards' before releasing a miniature parachutist to float gently back to earth. (What happened to the rocket is not recorded.) (Hulton Getty)

a series and Sooty was soon the must-have toy for the new generation of TV-watching children.

'Television has been the means of introducing to the family circle a collection of animal friends who are rapidly gaining extreme popularity with all viewing children,' wrote a contemporary TV critic. Among the alternatives to Sooty were Mr Turnip, Muffin the Mule, Sally Seal, Oswald Ostrich and Poppy Parrot – some of whom are long forgotten. But the critic had the foresight to pick out the most memorable. 'Muffin will undoubtedly, eventually, become an international figure and a Muffin Syndicate is already in place to fully exploit the commercial possibilities.'

Star endorsement was available from the BBC's *Watch with Mother* team. Alongside Flowerpot Men painting books and Andy Pandy jigsaw puzzles, the latest hollow-cast metal toys included an Andy Pandy and a Flowerpot Men set which included Weed and two des. res. pots for the prattling puppets.

Toy firms may have spotted the potential of TV, but there was a long way to go to achieve nationwide saturation. In 1952 a fourteen-inch black-and-white TV cost a princely seventy-two guineas – about six weeks' wages for most people – and a few years would pass before a fall in prices made them a standard feature in every home, and a channel for direct sales pitches to every child's world.

But things certainly were changing, and even the rituals of Christmas, for so long unchanged, were beginning to be coloured by the excitement of the new. Kids expected more. An old guy with a white beard in a red coat just wasn't enough for many of them, and they demanded something more up to date. Shops pulled out all the stops to oblige. For Christmas 1955 at Arding & Hobbs, Santa arrived in a Wild West stage-coach, while at John Lewis in Oxford Street he turned up in a fifty-foot express loco, to join guest celebrity James Robertson Justice. The latter event attracted so many people that things quickly dissolved into chaos and the bearded star of the *Doctor* films had to carry Santa upstairs to the sanctuary of his grotto. At Roomes store in Upminster the white-bearded one arrived in a vintage 1905 car. At Dixons in Southend he turned up by train at the local railway station, from whence he was whisked into town in a hired 1911 Model T. It was left to the Willesden Co-op in north London to make a stand for traditional values, with dear Santa arriving at the reins of an old-fashioned sleigh.

Even the grottoes were less grotty. The one at Dunning's in Maidstone was transmuted into Father Neptune's Undersea Castle. At Jones & Higgins in Peckham the bearded one sat in a Flying Saucer while in Cardiff he held court on his very own Treasure Island. At Bonds of Chelmsford the poor old gent had to make do with a 'Christmas caravan'. Again it was the Co-op – this time in Leytonstone – that stood firm for the old values with their simple 'Snowland' set up.

Many Santa Clauses, in America at least, were former winos. Christmas grottoes were often set up under the auspices of charity groups, and profits ploughed back into projects in the Bowery and various prisons. Down-and-outs were given a chance to redeem themselves by playing Father Christmas. The regulation fluffy white beard may have been false, but the red cheeks and nose were often authentic enough. Recidivists were not tolerated. Any man found breathing Jack Daniels fumes into the faces of expectant tots was automatically removed from ho-ho-hoing duties.

My Christmases, as I recall them, were brilliant. I was blessed with numerous aunties and uncles – not to mention my mother's work colleagues – who showered me with presents. One Christmas morning, aged seven or eight, I was awakened by a dozy awareness of a great weight pressing on my legs. Raising a sleepy head I was astonished to see my blue eider-down spread with an awesome array – literally sacks full of toys, plus a stocking or two bulging with assorted oranges and nuts, a chocolate Santa Claus and a massive pink sugar pig.

We all have our fond memories. Mine wouldn't be the same as yours, but it's likely they include a few of the same things: a wooden fort, painted white and red; a garage made of tinplate, with a real working lift for moving the toy cars up to the first floor. The cars and soldiers were too numerous to recall, though for some reason I can specifically remember two cowboy figures and the names I gave them – Stone and Pick; Stone was mustard-yellow plastic and sported a lasso. My favourite lorry was a huge tin-plate truck which came complete with two large cable drums made of real wood loaded on the back. Painted green and red, the lorry had marvellous chunky wheels. It's the wheels I remember most of all, which perhaps goes to show that it's the sensual, textural nature of our toys that remains in our memories the longest.

In addition to these big toys I was presented with all manner of fascinating side dishes, miscellaneous odds and ends that I'd never have thought of asking for, even if I'd known they existed. Like a solitaire game with coloured plastic pegs, contained in a neat plastic case that closed with a satisfying snap. I never learned to play the game, but I prized the case for ages. There was a wooden dominoes set (which I still have), a chess set, bagatelle, and handheld flat plastic maze around which one had to manoeuvre a blob of mercury to the centre without it breaking and scattering in all directions. Some of the toys were even more basic – like Twirlo, just a round piece of card threaded on a string that produced a whirring noise when spun around – very similar to the Everlasting Catherine Wheel from the 1920s.

Since they're now usually sold in B & Q and Do It All, I've never been entirely convinced that torches really count as toys. Still, they were *de rigueur* for most boys my age, and if we used them in our games then I suppose they must count as toys. As well as the standard-issue hand-held ones, with filters to switch the light from white to green to red, I had a fantastic copper-coloured one designed like a storm lantern, with a domed red light on the top and a powerful front-projected beam. What most boys aspired to was one of the massive rubber-sleeved torches – as used by policemen, spies and burglars – the sort that had a mile-long beam and could be used to guide a helicopter landing. Unfortunately, such magnificent accessories were well beyond our means...

Yesterday's children always enjoyed dual nationality, access to another country, a realm within a realm that their parents were hardly aware of, a land of dumps and allotments and ponds. Our territory consisted of an acre or two of hillocky ground criss-crossed by ash paths and bordered with railway sidings where condemned carriages waited for disposal, every one of their windows smashed, their maroon seats covered in glittering showers of glass. Our parallel world was packed with adventures but, let's face it, must have been a constant worry for our mothers. And as if broken glass, rusting cars and stagnant ponds weren't enough, the very ground we walked on was a fire hazard. If you dug down into the conglomerate of ash, stones and earth smoke would begin to rise out of it. To this day I don't know why it was there or how it came to be there, but there was a glowing incandescence slowly and inexorably burning its way through the earth beneath our feet.

A rough and ready land, for sure, but it had a completely integrated transport system, with wheels to suit every budget: improvised trolleys made of discarded pram wheels, smart scooters, tinny-looking skates and splendid bikes which were often given as reward for a pass in the eleven-plus exam. Bikes were status symbols and it was a great day when the rider pro-gressed from one of the numerous kiddies' models – such as the Defiant Junior, with its 'protected driver's mechanism' to stop you falling off – to a real racer. But these were well out of the reach of most kids of the fifties.

If Henry Ford had ever been in the scooter business he'd probably have said, 'Sure, kid, choose any colour you like – as long as it's red.' Before their recent resurgence did you ever see a scooter that wasn't? A cheerful fire-engine red, admittedly, often splendorised by yellow or black handle grips, but still red, forever and unrepentantly red. Mobo and Tri-ang were the big names, rivals who didn't even have the sense to compete in opposing colours. If they had, kids could have used their brand loyalty to stage an update of their Cowboys and Indians games – the Mobos vs the Tri-angs.

Despite being a majority, scooter riders could never shake off their inferiority complex. Kids who possessed bikes were envied as they posed at the kerbside to show off their Sturmey-Archer gears, glittering whirl of spokes, the tape of their handle-bars. Glamour and cool were qualities absent from scooters in those days. Yet, for all that, they had a certain haughty eccen-tricity. They seemed to belong to that surreal England of penny-farthings and bath-chairs, zany transport options for a nation of nutcases. Scooters might well have been dreamed up by an apprentice of Heath-Robinson, fired by his mentor's visions, but not quite skilled enough to tackle anything with pulleys and cogs. Hence the scooter, which must have at least earned him an encouraging pat on the back from his master.

Some clever marketing must have been afoot here (although perhaps not in the same league as the genius who convinced a generation of children in 2000, who could have had 'anything' compared to us in the fifties, that what they really *had* to have was a scooter). How else could otherwise prudent (and much less wealthy) parents be coerced into buying their kiddies a toy that had no sensible function? Practical uses for a scooter were and are severely limited. You can't really go to school on it, you can't take a spin in the country with it. Scooters have a severely short range. No one wants to scoot for longer than five minutes. You are half-knackered before you get to the end of the street. They don't even have a saddlebag for fetching a bottle of pop from the shops.

As parents of today are discovering, while bicycles can at least claim to save shoe leather, scooters erode it. No pair of shoes would stand a school holiday's worth of heavy scooter-ing. Or rather, one shoe remains pristine and pampered and aloof, while the other is an exhausted lackey. It's as if the class war is being acted out by shoes – one the pampered idler, the other wearing itself ragged earning a living.

The most sophisticated scooters, like their modern equiva-lents, boasted brakes. Or rather a brake: a spring-loaded sprug that pressed down on the back wheel. As every scooterist knows, this is considerably less effective than simply jumping off. And apart from the occasional kamikaze hot-head, how many children ever work up enough speed to need brakes?

Scooters are similarly useless for escaping from bullies. Any fleet-of-foot teenage bully can outstrip a scooter. The scooter's weak point will always be its rider. For want of a shoelace the battle is so often lost, or a trainer with a flapping sole, or even a slipper which flies off, and is picked up by the bully who can now sit and wait for his 'Cinderella' to return for a mandatory Chinese burn or dead-leg.

Mums dusting their windowsills are now no doubt becoming reacquainted with the sight of a phantom scooter whizzing past down the street. Little Johnny's scooter with a life of its own. What could it mean? Some kind of spooky sign? The chrome equivalent of a faithful hound returning home to report its master's fate? No, it's just that the owner has discovered inertia. With the right technique a scooter can run for many yards entirely unaided and fierce competition develops to see who can send their scooter furthest. Parents who witness this craze in action are furious – it's clearly no way to treat an expensive toy – not understanding that it's all part of the fun.

Scooters remained popular throughout the fifties and sixties, but then disappeared for thirty years prior to their unexpected resurgence. The disappearance makes a good deal more sense than the reappearance, because they always felt a bit too much like hard work. For those without a bike of their own – I was thirteen before I got my first – the transport to aspire to was a trolley. Like cars, trolleys conferred status. You had a trolley and you were someone – or at least a junior someone. Trolleys took many forms, from the sadly inept to well-made vehicles constructed by indulgent dads with proper steering, nuts, bolts and textbook design. First you had to find your wheels. On the dumps and wasteground where we played it was easy enough, since they turned up with useful regularity. One wasn't much good, but a set of two was always worth having. Lucky scavengers might come across an integrated set of four pram wheels, still attached to the chassis. A basic trolley could be formed by simply adding a strong box to the four wheels and being satisfied with that. More impressive were 'stretch' trolleys, formed with a plank and two sets of four wheels, a real limousine among trolleys.

Pram wheels, though, are not the most sturdy of rollers. Get two overweight boys on a weak axle and the whole thing bust. End of trolley. End of wheels. Back to scavenging the dumps again and if they didn't produce the goods perhaps some petty larceny would. While I don't recall any babies being kidnapped, there were reports of pushchairs being stolen from outside shops or from people's backyards and being broken up for their wheels.

The biggest drawback to the trolley, of course, was motive power. Slaves or willing volunteers were needed. Sometimes it was compulsory, younger children being press-ganged into providing the puff. Mostly, though, it worked on a reciprocal basis – if you consented to provide push power, the trolley's owner would usually be decent enough to give you a go on it while he did the same for you.

A new form of mobility was provided by Terraglide, single-track roller-skates 'for gliding, dancing, figure-skating and hockey'. Advertised as 'super silent', they had spherical rubber wheels which were supposedly ideal for steep-angle banking and skidding.

For real eccentricity, though, Jumping Jacks were hard to beat. Fashioned like roller-skates, the JJs had springs instead of wheels. More or less a revival of the 1930s Kangru Springshus, the JJs were not so much ground-breaking as ankle-breaking, at least for those children who failed to master the correct jumping technique.

I can't let this golden age pass without mention of my dolls. Rather like Judas betraying Jesus, boys tend to deny the existence of their dolls, but I had several over a period of years and I feel duty-bound to give them a mention in dispatches. There was the obligatory golliwog, a fluffy Scotty dog and a rag-doll figure of Mr Force, jaunty figurehead of an early breakfast cereal, which my mum acquired in return for a one-shilling postal order and innumerable packet tops.

A favourite doll...well, more of a hot-water bottle with attitude, went by the name of Dolly Daydream. I walked

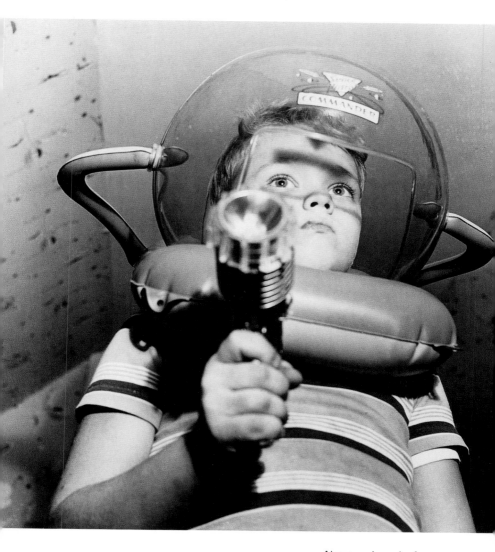

Above and overleaf:
Space-age mania
swept the States
and Britain in the
fifties (*Hulton Getty,
Robert Opie
Collection & V&A*)

Subbuteo set from 1955
(*Robert Opie Collection*)

Die-cast model buses from the seventies

Lego, the toy of the
century, according
to a recent Internet
poll (*Robert Opie
Collection*)

By the seventies TV & sports tie-ins were commonplace in toy marketing (*both Robert Opie Collection*)

Barbie, from the sixties
to the eighties (*Robert
Opie Collection & V&A*)

around with Dolly as a constant companion. One day, while holding her, I fell in the local brook. It was a horrid, panicky experience – the coldness and enveloping murkiness of the water, the taste of dead sticklebacks and frog spawn. A man on the nearby allotments rushed over to pull me out, but Dolly was gone, sunk in the depths of the brook, all two feet of them. The man was too set on getting me home to Mum to bother about my insane twitterings about Dolly Daydream. He probably thought I was delirious.

The day afterwards I went back to look. I peered into the water and poked a stick around among the weeds: no sign of dear drowned Dolly. One of the older boys took pity on me. He explained that the hottie had probably been washed downstream, but since there was a grille where the brook passed under the railway, it was odds on that Dolly would be waiting for me there. Encouraged, I followed him along the path, all the while peering into the water for a sign. Skirting the allotments, we came to the grille, but there was no sign of Dolly, just a mass of dark, oil-clogged water on which floated a collection of corks and pop bottles and a plastic gun. Above us a train bound for Derby let out a mournful wet whistle. It was the saddest let-down of my little life.

And there was Noddy, of course. He was my favourite and knocked around in my bedroom well into the sixties and my early teens, a guest of honour sitting out his retirement among an assortment of *Railway World*s and *Melody Maker*s. Noddy took it all in his stride, though he might have decided to quit when he caught sight of my new black-and-white checked hipsters bought specially for a Hollies, Spencer Davis and Tremeloes concert at Leicester De Montfort Hall.

Oh, Noddy! Bitter is my regret. How we turn on our most faithful companions. One day, as I was dancing frenziedly to *Get Off Of My Cloud* by the Rolling Stones I was seized by madness. Blood lust almost. I grabbed Noddy from his resting place and shook him and whirled him in time to the music, dancing and dancing, getting crazier and crazier on the beat, until ecstasy turned to anger and thinking how ridiculous

Noddy was in my new world of teenage rebellion I ripped at his amiable rubberised face until half of it was gone. How could anyone have done such a thing to such an amiable icon? The damage was too severe to repair. 'Multiple injuries' is the delicate term used by the press. For days afterwards I felt awful. I wouldn't even let my mum see what I'd done. Though I could never nurse him back to health I tried to keep him in comfortable indolence in a drawer full of Y-fronts. But every time I changed for school I was caught out by his reproachful war veteran's look. His jolliness had gone and there was a look of madness in his remaining eye.

1960s

The 1960s: decade of innovation and revolution. But some things just refuse to go away. Take, for instance, the pogo stick. Having wowed the twenties and the forties it was now ready for the sixties, albeit with some hi-tech improvements. The Combustible Gas Powered Pogo Stick was patented by Gordon Spitzmesser from Indiana. His pogo stick was, in essence, a small gasoline motor. The piston connecting rod was the foot of the pogo stick, and the bouncing action fired the spark plug through a magneto. Fill the tank, turn on the switch, and bounce ... and bounce higher ... and higher ... It wasn't the first such idea: that was the 'Mechanical Jumping Stick', patented in 1950 and marketed for a brief period in the early sixties by the aptly named Chance Manufacturing of Wichita, under the trademark Hop Rod. The firm even staged publicity pre-race Hop Rod events at the Indianapolis 500.

'If you maintained a forward leaning position you could really cover some ground,' said one Hop Rod veteran. There was a rumour going around that Goodyear racing tyre engineers had redesigned the device and, with special fuel, were getting twelve feet per hop! The harder one jumped, the higher the compression and greater uptake of fuel, and the bigger the pop. A good sense of balance was essential, as the Hop Rod still worked if you came down at an angle, resulting in you being propelled sideways, at great speed and with no hope of recovery. A TV personality tried one live on air, tilted and was catapulted on to his desk, breaking his collarbone and wrist. Several similar incidents led to a ban by the Department of Transportation and the Hop Rods are no longer commercially available because of the obvious dangers. Those who

Wheels in the sixties
(Mary Evans Picture Library)

sampled the joys likened the experience to riding a runaway pneumatic drill without anything to tether it.

A much gentler pursuit was Pretzel. In 1965 Reyn Guyer, its inventor, managed a sales-promotion firm specialising in store displays and package design for companies like Pillsbury, 3M and Kraft. Commissioned by a shoe-polish firm to create a promotional gift, Guyer came up with an idea that involved coloured patches that went on kids' feet, with corresponding colours on a walkaround grid. It quickly occurred to him that it could be the basis for a game, and after getting the company artists to sketch out a giant board, he organised a trial run with two teams of workers from the office. Seeing the fun that ensued, Guyer worked on the idea and it evolved into Pretzel. The idea was eventually sold to the Milton Bradley company who, against Guyer's wishes, changed the name to Twister.

Retailers were somewhat wary of Twister, unsure what category to put it in and doubting whether people would even understand the rules. When the game finally hit the shops in 1966 critics and competitors were quick to accuse the company of selling 'sex in a box'. There had never been a game which encouraged so much body contact. The possibilities were endless and unthinkable: in a frenetic game of Twister brothers could find themselves nose to bosom with their sisters, daughters could end up staring at their father's crotch, sons could be looking right down their mother's cleavage. With moral reservations like these, Milton Bradley became increasingly doubtful about its chances of success. But fear of widespread public criticism was soon obliterated when the game was demonstrated by Johnny Carson on his popular *Tonight* show. One of his guests that night was Eva Gabor, wearing a low-cut gown. With Eva splayed out on all fours on the polkadot Twister mat, Johnny twirled the spinner and took his turn. As he climbed on top of Eva, the studio audience went into joyous hysterics. With such star endorsement Milton Bradley knew they had a huge hit on their hands. More than three million Twisters were sold during its first year. Undisputed king of sixties game fads, Twister brought a new meaning to the phrase 'contact sports', and the game was a big hit on college campuses.

Rival companies soon came up with variations, such as Parker Brothers' Funny Bones, a card-based game where each card came with instructions from the old nursery rhyme, commands such as 'head bone connected to the elbow', or 'back bone connected to the hand bone'. Players did as instructed on their cards, often resulting in comical poses.

While the adults contorted themselves, their daughters were about to be beguiled by a doll whose lack of any sort of flexibility seemed to matter not one jot to its legions of devotees. At the end of the 1950s, noticing how her daughter was fascinated by cut-out paper dolls with interchangeable sets of clothes, Mattel executive Ruth Handler suggested making a three-dimensional doll through which little girls could act out their dreams. She named the doll 'Barbie' – the nickname of her daughter. The first Barbie sported a ponytail hairstyle, black-and-white bathing suit, open-toed shoes, sunglasses and earrings, and came with a range of fashion accessories.

This glamorous and yet somehow sanitised beauty was allegedly based on Lilli, a frisky fraulein in a German newspaper cartoon aimed squarely at adult males. Whatever the truth, Barbie was one of the first dolls to have a distinctly grown-up figure and obvious sexuality, unlike most dolls at that time which were still primarily based on dubious cherubim and possessed distinctly sexless features.

Buyers at the New York Toy Fair may not have been overly impressed, but little girls certainly were and the Barbie doll took American toyshops by storm. Barbie's success was so rapid that Mattel become a publicly owned company in 1960.

Originally intended as a teenage fashion model, over the ensuing years Barbie has taken on a variety of aspirational roles and tackled almost every conceivable profession, from doctor and firefighter to astronaut and presidential candidate. Friends and family have joined her over the years, including Ken – named after the Handlers' son – in 1961, Midge in 1963 and Skipper in 1965. Christie, an Afro-American doll and the first of many ethnic friends, joined the Barbie set in 1968.

Backed by TV advertising, Barbie was destined for huge worldwide success and was selling so quickly that the Mattel factory could not keep up with demand.

Mattel had its origins in 1945 when founders Harold Matson and Elliot Handler began operating out of a garage workshop. Their original business was making picture frames, but Handler soon developed a sideline in dolls' house furniture made from the leftover scraps of wood. After Matson sold up, Elliot and his wife, Ruth, encouraged by the success of the dolls' house furniture, turned the company's emphasis to toys. The Uke-a-Doodle, a child-size ukulele, was the first in a line of musical toys, and a hand-cranked music-box gave them their first 'staple' business. In 1955, Mattel introduced the Burp Gun, a patented automatic cap gun, and the same year, in a move that revolutionised the way toys were marketed, the Handlers bought fifty-two weeks of advertising on the new *Mickey Mouse Club* TV show, the first time toys had been advertised so continually and repetitively.

As a direct result of the high profile their sponsorship won them, Mattel's next line, the child-size Mouseguitar, became an instant success. These musical toys were soon followed by replica rifles and guns. Healthy sales reflected the popularity of

Western shows like *Bonanza*, *Gunsmoke* and *The Lone Ranger* and – with wonderful symbiosis – these same programmes served as a continual free advert for Mattel's growing range of cowboy games, dolls and guns.

Sindy, Britain's answer to Barbie, first appeared in 1963. British girls took to her with equal rapture, though it seems they could be just as entranced by Gonks and Trolls, ugly squat figures with bright punk-style hair that were being heavily endorsed by Diana Dors.

While the girls fussed over their dolls, their brothers were wreaking havoc with small but solid lumps of metal. Die-cast toy cars had originally been designed as peripherals to model railways. By the 1960s they had certainly come to be toys in their own right and newcomer Corgi was zooming into the lead. Corgi's great strength was its innovation, a policy which led Dinky and Matchbox to follow suit to the benefit of every-one. Not all their gimmicks were successful, but for every one that failed Corgi had a dozen that took off.

In the 1930s Philipp Ullman had arrived at Winteringham's in Northampton, bringing with him twenty-one years of experience in the toy industry. He teamed up with Arthur Katz and their first tin-plate models formed the basis of the company which became Mettoy Limited. Mettoy seceded from Winteringham's in 1936.

Due to wartime restrictions on toy-making the company turned to producing shells and mortar carriers. In 1944, as a result of ever-increasing demand, the firm moved to larger premises in Swansea, and following further expansion the new Mettoy factory was officially opened in April 1949.

Forerunners of Corgi cars appeared in the firm's illustrated catalogue as 'Entirely New Miniature Numbers'. In 1954 the first drawings for the new Corgi range were produced. Mettoy knew that to copy the Dinky product would not be enough to guarantee success so all vehicles in the Corgi range would boast windows, 'The First with Windows' becoming one of the early slogans. The Corgi Austin Cambridge finally rolled off its miniature production line on 9 July 1956, after a period of trial and error with castings.

Following the example of Meccano and other manufacturers, the Corgi Model Club and a regular newsletter were established. The first proper catalogue followed in 1957 and the firm started advertising on TV. Sales for the first year reached an amazing 2.75 million pieces. Innovations continued with the launch of the Renault Floride, which featured not only windows but seats and panelling, steering-wheel and spring suspension, features which soon became standard on all Corgi models.

The firm was well into its stride by now and was adept at marketing. Playing the publicity game to the hilt, their model Bluebird Record car was presented to Donald Campbell prior to his latest record attempt in the USA. By the mid-1960s Corgi models were selling to the tune of 17 million a year and the company picked up two Queen's Awards for Industry. Mettoy became a public company and in a reflection of its success, the share issue was oversubscribed by two and a half times.

The 1960 hovercraft was a timely and popular model and stood on three individually sprung ballbearings. In 1961 came a tractor with a vibrating exhaust stack and, most pleasing of all, jewelled headlights. The BRM Grand Prix had a driver, a Union Jack decal on the roof and small round stickers on the wheels to feign spoked wheels. By 1962 there were licence plates, spokes, whitewalls, and car boots with tiny suitcases inside and bonnets that opened to reveal engines. At the 1964 Motor Show, Corgi brought out a Mercedes limousine with working windscreen wipers, while the Mini was one of the must-have toys, since it came out just a couple of years after the real thing. There'd always been a commercial dimension to many of the toys – the Co-op pop lorry, Chipperfields' Circus trucks (complete with giraffes, camels and lions) and a Walls ice-cream van that featured a crank at the rear to make the chimes work! But it was TV and cinema that was destined to exert the greatest influence on toy cars.

The James Bond 007 Aston Martin DB5, issued in 1965, was a replica of the car which made its first appearance in *Goldfinger* the previous year. Showing amazing ingenuity and attention to detail, the car featured projecting rams, guns, a bullet shield and, of course, an ejector seat that fired its hapless plastic passenger through a roof. The car electrified the toy world, bringing publicity, prestige and increased business to Corgi.

Hot on the heels of the James Bond success came models based on vehicles seen in *Batman*, *Daktari* (this one came complete with cross-eyed lion!) and *Man from UNCLE*. There was a wonderful *Avengers* two-piece set featuring Steed's Bentley and Emma Peel's Lotus. To counter accusations that Corgi were straying too far from traditional values, 1967 also saw the appearance of another Bentley, driven by Jeeves and with a figure of Bertie Wooster in languid leaning pose.

A change of scale came in 1967, from 1:48 to the European standard of 1:43, thereby removing the toys even further from their old relationship to model railway land. Chitty Chitty Bang Bang (with retractable wings), released in 1968, certainly had no place in the car park of any British Rail station in the sixties! There was a definite shift away from realism now and 1969 saw the arrival of the Monkeemobile, Noddy's car and the Beatles' Yellow Submarine. The next decade saw even more commercial tie-ins: a Coca-Cola van, Charlie's Angels van, Fred Flintstone's Flyer, Barney's Buggy, not forgetting Wilma's own palaeolithic runaround, for the Flintstones were, of course, a two-log family. A curious one-off gift set was Eight Lions of Longleat, complete with plastic joints of meat.

Despite the high profile in the toyshops, Corgi's fortunes nosedived in 1969 when a fire gutted the company's warehouse and a year's stock of models was destroyed. The resulting backlog forced many toyshops to turn back to Dinky, a blip which caused some damage to Corgi's fortunes. By the 1970s, with competition from the USA added to their woes, Mettoy was forced to shed 900 workers and to save the day a distribution agreement was entered into with Fisher-Price.

But Dinky wasn't short of ideas of its own. It had already produced an armoured car stacked with mini-gold bullion bars and *Dinky's* Aston Martin had real wire spokes, opening doors and bonnet, tipping seats, dashboard and gears (but no ejector

Dinky toy Land Rover from the sixties

seat). The company was also not slow to cash in on the trend for TV-slanted toys. In 1967 three ground-breaking Dinky toys, both allied to television programmes, were introduced. The first was *Fab 1*, Lady Penelope's Rolls-Royce. Despite its finish of girly pink, the car was capable of a no-nonsense response by launching a rocket at potential enemies. Following close behind – prudently not within rocket-firing distance – came *Thunderbird 2* and Captain Scarlet's *Spectrum* Pursuit Vehicle. A toy Spitfire aeroplane was issued to coincide with the film *Battle of Britain*; its propeller could be fitted with an electric motor.

As these examples show, children were making increasingly sophisticated demands of their toys, and cars especially were expected to keep pace with all the developments in motoring. Speedwheels – first fitted to Dinky's Pontiac Parisienne – had been designed to give a smoother, longer-lasting roll than anything before. This was followed by Dragster, whose starter unit was fitted with a spring to send the sporty racer on its way.

But the biggest development was the introduction of

Mattel's Hot Wheels in 1968. Two years earlier, Elliot and Ruth Handler, the co-founders of Mattel, set out to develop a die-cast car that was better than the foreign versions their grandchildren loved to play with. The team assembled for the project at Mattel's California HQ included a US Navy missile engineer and Harry Bradley, one of General Motors' designers. 'Man, those are some hot wheels!' Elliot Handler is reputed to have said when he saw Bradley's classic Southern California hot rod in the parking lot. And so the Hot Wheels brand name was born, combining the hot-rod theme with improved suspension and wheel design.

Once they had reinvented the wheel, the design team moved on to the body. During the sixties, the California hot rod was all the rage and, inspired by this craze, the Hot Wheels team employed the same exciting paint jobs and customisation details. Sixteen different Hot Wheels models were produced in 1968, selling for a very affordable fifty-nine cents apiece. Their success was instant and they soon crossed the Atlantic to burn off the competition in British toyshops.

Other gimmicks weren't so successful. Golden Jacks, introduced in 1968, were cars with detachable wheels (why?). The car sat there, unmoving, on its 'golden jacks'. The huge number of wheels that predictably became lost is probably what led to the idea being phased out two years later.

But fiddly little pieces of easily lost plastic seemed to be strangely appealing to toy manufacturers in the sixties. Witness Mousetrap. There was (still is) an axiom in the business world – 'build a better mousetrap and the world will beat a path to your door' – but this mousetrap must have been one of the most unnecessarily complicated devices than any inventor had devised. Nevertheless, everyone loved it. It was a clever combination of board game and constructional toy and its Heath-Robinson battiness made it irresistible to children and adults alike.

Then there was Bayko. By the time Meccano took it over in 1960, Bayko was a once-popular brand in decline. First introduced in 1934, it was invented by the owner of the Plimpton Engineering Company in Liverpool. The idea was simple enough: plastic pieces representing bricks, windows, pillars, doors and roofs which were slid into place between rods inserted into a perforated base. Sets included screws, nuts, rods and connectors (plenty of things to lose there, then!) – and a handy screwdriver. Conversion sets were available in the manner pioneered by Meccano, with sets 1a to 4a turning set 1 to set 2, set 2 to set 3 and so on. The first sets, available in five sizes, were fashioned in Bakelite and featured large brown bases, white and brown bricks, maroon roofs and dark green doors and windows. There were also steps, chimneys and canopies. The brown bricks were later changed to a more attractive red. Bayko wasn't, like the Lego that eventually ousted it in popularity, just a matter of snapping two bricks together. You needed a base and a planned skeleton of steel rods, and only then did you slot in your brick sections. Even then you had to remember basics such as joists at the corners and over the windows.

Bayko enjoyed widespread public exposure and the British Industries Fair featured a magnificent model village made entirely from it, as well as a skyscraper which stood over six feet tall. It was unashamedly aspirational: no one wanted to build a plebby terraced house – these were exec-style habitats. As well as bay windows and pebbledash you could add that final flourish to your front door with a pair of white pillars. Bayko was a quaint reminder of a middle England that never quite existed in reality. Well, maybe it did – down south – but there were certainly no houses as grand around our part of the industrial Midlands. It dated back to a heyday before the Second World War and its houses spoke of a prosperous Home Counties life. Yet we provincials took to them with a kind of instinct that they represented the rewards of a steady job and a compulsory suit. Porches and pillars, bay windows and gables; these were houses with style. Yet whatever the class analysis, Bayko provided a basic grounding in house construction. We may not get to live in houses like these, but we might well end up carrying the hods of bricks to make them!

By 1959, more new parts had been added to keep pace with

the changing social trends of Macmillan's Britain: Bayko houses could now boast garage doors, TV aerials and ramps. But competition from the Danish Lego was beginning to affect Bayko's sales and in 1960 Meccano made its move. The new owners promptly set about redesigning every part. They also switched colour schemes and – worst of all for many – changed the materials to plastic. Window glazing was also introduced, though Plimpton had probably been considering this innovation themselves.

Bayko's colour scheme lent the young property developer's enterprise a slightly surreal look: respectable semis and detached houses constructed in bright reds and greens, not day-glo enough to be freaky, but distinctive enough to look decidedly at odds with the real world. Or perhaps, I imagined at the time, there really was some *Twilight Zone* town in the south of England constructed entirely in bold shades of red and green.

Away from the home front, but still relentlessly upwardly mobile, instruction booklets suggested modest projects such as a five-storey hotel or a country club – the latter being six feet in length! But it wasn't all grandiose architecture: there were options to build garages, lean-tos and sheds (presumably for the staff).

The competition in the toy construction market in the sixties seems remarkable when viewed from our Lego-dominated times. As well as Bayko there was Cliki, building sets based on interlocking plastic blocks which enabled the construction of small houses; toy houses, that is (though it's quite conceivable that a boy with enough sets might build a full-size habitat for his family). Cliki blocks bore a remarkable resemblance to Lego but ultimately could not challenge the Danish supremacy.

The same was true for Plastic Meccano, introduced in 1965, and extra large to enable stubby little fingers to grasp, literally, the basic principles of building a suspension bridge or crane. In 1968 Meccano also made miniature sewing-machines – for girls, of course. The electrically operated Jones-Meccano produced a lockstitch and was priced at nine pounds. And years before Thomas the Tank Engine came to dominate the lovable loco market, Meccano issued a Percy train set, also based on characters from the Reverend Awdry's railway books.

Unfortunately for Meccano, even these late changes failed to stem the Lego invasion and it was the beginning of the end for Bayko. By 1967 it was on its last legs, though stocks could be bought in toyshops until 1969. Meccano's own export turnover was a healthy £1 million, yet the company reported an interim loss of nearly £29,000, attributed to a global recession in train sets coupled with (definitely not my pun!) a reluctance to increase retail prices because of competition. As the deficit rose, sweeping management restructuring and premises changes were required, but with profits looking unlikely, Meccano advised its shareholders to accept a takeover offer from the Lines Group. The company became Meccano-Tri-ang. The Hornby name was phased out and the machine tools sold to Wrenn, another Lines Group subsidiary. Unfortunately for Lines, a lack of promised investment from the USA forced them into liquidation. Assets were transferred to a new company, Meccano (1971) Ltd, and then, simply as Meccano Ltd, the newly profitable company was sold to Airfix. The Hornby name was sold to Rovex, who manufactured Tri-ang trains sets.

With all this demand for construction toys, it's hardly surprising that a toy which enabled junior draughtsmen to make blueprint after blueprint also emerged in the sixties. Etch-A-Sketch was invented by Paul Chasse, a Parisian mechanic with a yen for tinkering. Usually restricted to cars, his talents were extended in 1958 to an automatic drawing toy – christened *L'Ecran Magique* – that needed no batteries and had no parts that could go wrong. A mixture of aluminium powder and plastic beads was used to coat the screen and a metal stylus, moved by the knobs, dislodged the grey mixture, causing lines to appear, much like using a finger to write on a misty window. A shake redistributes the mixture and the lines disappear.

The 'magic screen' excited great interest when first demonstrated in Germany, but it was rejected by all the manufacturers who saw it – mainly because Chasse wanted an unthinkable amount of money for the rights on an unproven toy. One firm who rejected it was Ohio Art, but when it was brought to their attention a second time they decided to risk the $25,000 that Chasse wanted for the licence. In 1960 the toy hit the shops as Etch-A-Sketch. Early production-line problems meant that one in four units were rejected – ending up in garbage dumps – where they were promptly pounced on by savvy scavengers who immediately took them back to shops and demanded a refund for their disappointing 'purchases'.

Less prone to such technical breakdown, the jigsaw puzzle still enjoyed a healthy profile. Many of the new ones, such as *Coronation Street*, *Burke's Law*, *Mighty Mole*, *Beverly Hillbillies*, *Z Cars* and *Dr Who* were cashing in on TV programmes, while a variety of up-to-date versions featured pop groups like the Beatles and the Rolling Stones. The manufacturers were full of optimism and went so far as to say that the one featuring Mick Jagger and co. would be one of the bestsellers in jigsaw history. Oddly enough, a few years later, the Stones penned a song called 'Jigsaw Puzzle' for the *Beggars Banquet* album.

Even the smallest children were not immune from pop music, and to cater to hip toddlers there were Rock Rhythm Nursery Rhyme discs featuring pun-driven cover versions such as 'Hickory Dickory Rock'. Would-be pop stars could acquire a gift pack of Rolling Stones maracas, 'As Played by Mick Jagger!' But so great was parental aversion to the Rolling Stones that they may well have preferred to buy their offspring the battery-operated pneumatic drill with real-life sound and cutter, rammer and chisel attachments... Noisier, admittedly, but no danger to public morals.

No manufacturer was ashamed to cash in on the latest trends. There was even a Meccano pop group, the Dinky Beats, 'all typical characters down to their long hair, lapel-less jackets and narrow trousers'.

Noise was certainly an issue, and toys must have been

getting rowdier. The secretary of the Noise Abatement Society, made a written request to the Louis Marx Company to ask if they would stop making battery-operated sound units that simulated the roar of a motorbike. The units could be clipped to the crossbar of a child's bicycle. The NAS was seeking legal advice, it claimed, but the silence of the toy companies and importers in response was as deafening as their sound units. 'V-rroom!' was another roar-maker imported from the United States. Those who couldn't afford one of these devices tried to keep up by using the time-honoured method of sticking a piece of cardboard between the wheel spokes.

But the biggest *bruit de jour* of all probably came from the legions of kids who were going around Britain's houses, backyards and streets squawking, 'Exterminate! Exterminate! Exterminate!' at ever-increasing pitch and volume. Despite Dr Who's best efforts, the Daleks had made a successful invasion of Planet Earth and captured the hearts of youngsters everywhere: 'Dalek devotion is younger children's answer to the Beatlemania of their older brothers and sisters,' opined the *Toy Trade Journal*. There were Daleks galore in all sizes, from the one-inch-high Dalek Rolykin priced at one shilling to the splendid battery-operated examples that blundered around the bedroom floor just like the real thing. Daleks added sci-fi kudos to everything from bagatelle games to jigsaw puzzles to spinning-tops. There was even an inflatable Dalek – though it looked far too daft to be really scary. The Dalek playsuit was made out of Storvic 120, a brand of PVC sheeting that was ideal for the job: it proudly claimed to be washable – unlike a real Dalek who would only rust in the rain.

Those who were fed up with the invaders might pester their parents for Dr Who's Anti-Dalek Neutron Exterminator. 'Fathers and other older members of the family may well recognise its similarity to the famous bazooka,' said the adverts, which seemed to be rather spoiling the game. 'Neutron exterminator? Get away with you! Me and Alf Perkins had one of them back in 1944! Did I ever tell you about the time we were dug in around Anzio ...?'

Before the good Doctor arrived in America (where he would similarly gain legions of fans) there was a TV show called *The Lieutenant*. This provided Hasbro with the inspiration for one of the more revolutionary ideas in the history of toys: a doll for boys. As soon as he was launched, GI Joe was an instant success.

Standing an impressive twelve inches tall, Joe sported a face which was a composite of the portraits of America's top twenty war heroes. He had a hard psychopathic stare and a facial scar in case anyone doubted his credentials. Joe's success came as a surprise to some toy-makers, who'd always assumed that boys wouldn't play with dolls while one writer claimed the whole idea of basing dolls upon war heroes was morally repugnant. The boys of America couldn't care less: Joe came with over a hundred accessories – guns, daggers and other death-dealing tools – and the boys loved it. GI Joe pulled in five million dollars in his first year.

'An end to war games please,' pleaded Suzy Menkes in *The Times*; Ann Kerr, a Labour MP expressed disgust at the sheer belligerence of the toy trade; at the Brighton Toy Fair there was a demo by the Women's International League for Peace and Freedom; Lady Antonia Fraser in her book *Toys* said, 'to get rid of war toys you first have to get rid of war. It's a microcosm, but not of the present. But why is a child's right to bear arms enshrined in nursery law?' An American group, PARTI, Parents for Responsibility in the Toy Industry, called for the manufacture of a toy dove with a built-in tape-recorder that would coo, 'Peace,' and various dolls with interlinking hands. 'We get used to the pathetic attempts of these ladies to ban war toys,' said a spokesman for the war-mongering toy-makers. 'But all the evidence shows that if a boy doesn't get the toy gun he wants, he simply goes out and finds a piece of wood and goes bang-bang.' 'It's good to let off steam,' said the famous childcare guru, Dr Spock, while a prison psychotherapist weighed in with his opinion that no correlation existed between toy guns and the real thing, even though he admitted that one convicted murderer had told him that when he shot his victim he'd expected him to get up again and was dismayed when he didn't.

Word of GI Joe's success soon reached the UK. British Xynolite, an associate company of Hasbro, decided to launch the doll in the UK as a Palitoy product. As it stood, the name GI Joe was far too American, so a manager suggested Action Man, after the very popular *Danger Man* TV series. Though he probably aspired to a VC, Action Man had to be content with the National Association of Toy Retailers' Toy of the Year Award. However, few people at the time could have imagined his longevity.

In 1968 the Talking Action Commander, capable of eight random commands, was introduced. Action Man sportsmen featured a footballer, cricketer and athlete. But it wasn't until the decade was over, in 1970, that Action Man was given 'realistic' flocked hair and a range of 'Adventurers' with beards were introduced as boxed figures. In 1973 Action Man sported gripping hands for the first time. The hands had a tendency to break if handled roughly and a thimble was provided to go over them while dressing the figure.

Along with the belligerent dolls, there seemed to be an unhealthy interest in physical injuries and body parts. Back in the toyshops of New York, one of the latest crazes was for one-eared Van Gogh dolls. Marybel, 'the doll that gets well', came with an array of splints, bandages and crutches. There were also adhesive pox spots which kiddies could apply and then remove with a flourish. Visible Man and Woman were two 'human anatomy kits' that came complete with all vital organs.

Those who were too inept for successful transplants might opt instead for Big Funeral, an American board game in which the winner was given a lavish funeral, while the losers were fated to become undead zombies. Presumably the zombies were banned from taking part in Live a Little, where the object was to murder the other players in order to collect their life insurance.

Toywise, for me the sixties were even better than the fifties. Variety and educational value I got in spades, though most of the more academic stuff tended to be a solo activity. I loved playing Cowboys and Indians as much as anyone, and I'd have been lost without my scooter, but I'd have been hard-pressed to find any other kid on the estate who'd share my enthusiasm for the erudite stuff. I wouldn't say it was a secret, it's just that I didn't bother telling anyone. When the scooter was safely parked in the garden shed and I went indoors, I threw off my scruffy-jumpered Just William act to adopt a more highbrow stance.

First of all there was the Junior Weather Station. Today it'd be called a Meteorological Discovery Centre. Does it even count as a toy? Well, it was bought for me one Christmas and it came from Toyland, our local toyshop, so I suppose it qualifies. It cost around seven guineas and came complete with a barometer, thermometer and anemometer. It seemed to be as sophisticated and wondrous as Mission Control at Cape Canaveral, except for the rain gauge which was suspiciously similar to Mum's Horlicks blender, just a glorified tumbler with measurements up the side. I supplemented the basic set by using some of my own pocket money to buy an extra maximum–minimum thermometer and my only regret is that I never worked out how to set up the anemometer. This caused great anguish, for the anemometer was the device that possessed the most instant charisma. I knew the Beaufort scale for measuring windspeed off by heart (a curious enough talent in a boy of nine) but 'leaves rustle' (4–7 m.p.h.), 'extends light flag' (8–12 m.p.h.) and 'raises loose paper' (13–18 m.p.h.) all seemed a bit too yokelly. I wanted technology, and to be the only kid on the estate with a personal anemometer was a status worth pursuing. But I couldn't do it, and I knew no one with the expertise to help. The barometer was fine, but tapping it every morning for a reading soon lost its novelty. I hankered after another dynamic instrument – a barograph, one of those amazing contraptions that drew a graph on a chart wrapped around a revolving drum – but such devices were for weather professionals or bourgeois show-offs and way beyond my five shillings pocket money!

'Boys will be boys, we understand, so you can be sure of a continuing market for Lotts Chemistry Sets.' The words date from the fifties, but the sentiments remained in the sixties. A chemistry set was one toy I never had – my mum considered them too dangerous – but my best friend had one. The give-away phrase is 'boys will be boys'. Despite what ambitious parents may have intended, it was highly unlikely that any boys intended to use Louis Pasteur or Robert Boyle as a role-model. More likely the inspiration came from Dennis the Menace or William Brown, as I proved on a visit to my friend's house. Far from performing innocuous experiments with litmus paper as recommended in the leaflet, I insisted on making stink bombs – to a samizdat formula that was available to any schoolkid. So successful was my experiment that the whole house was quickly enveloped in the grossest of chemical smells. I'd acci-dentally improved on the standard formula and if I hadn't been summarily ejected from the house by my friend's parents, I'd have had time to review my methodology. It was the stink-bomb equivalent of Big Boy and joke companies would surely have paid handsomely for the rights. The effects may have been more enduring than I'd planned, though, because the ban from visiting my friend wasn't lifted for two years. Maybe it's just as well that the formula now lies lost in the dusts of nostalgia.

Microscopes remain popular and you can still find them in Toys R Us, sharing shelf space alongside dolls, trikes and sets of Mousetrap. Most now come with a battery to make them seem hi-tech, but mine had only a mirror, which had to be carefully angled to reflect the necessary light. Along with the microscope I had a handsome wooden box into which to slot my slides, plus a variety of strange chemicals such as Canadian balsam. With a microscope the world was your bacillus. Bugs' legs, cross-sections of rhubarb, longitudinal sections of cherrywood, flies' wings – anything, err, microscopic would do for my collection.

Lancaster & Thorpe wasn't a toyshop. Although it sounds like a firm of solicitors, it was an optician's. It's still in business today, very much in the slick, brightly lit Specsavers mode now and staffed by efficient people in white coats. When I was young it had a far more intriguing ambience, and alongside the spectacles the shop sold telescopes, barometers and all kinds of associated paraphernalia. I was a regular visitor, and probably their youngest.

'Have you got a grasshopper's back leg?'

It wasn't cheek. Instead of clipping my ear, the lady assistant would duck behind a curtain into a back room, and odds-on she had the very leg in question. For in addition to its racks of monocles and horn-rimmed specs, Lancaster & Thorpe offered a selection of ready-made microscope slides with all manner of botanical cross-sections and insect segments. They weren't kept in the shop, obviously, in case short-sighted customers mistook them for signs of infestation. To their credit, the assistants even knew what Canadian balsam was.

Making your own slides worked out far cheaper. One of my hairs could look like a transatlantic telephone cable. Grains of salt, a speck of Colman's mustard powder, a teardrop of vinegar – Mum's kitchen cupboard also provided a great source of specimens. To her disgust, I even took samples from my meals: magnified and illuminated, a fragment of a Kellogg's Frostie resembled a splendid crystalline rock formation. But it wasn't all so rewarding: a drop of Heinz chicken soup was just a baffling yellow murk!

Another great source for me was the brook that ran along at the back of our house, the final resting-place of Dolly Daydream. I only had to clamber over the fence and jump down the bank to fetch a seaside bucket full of murky water. Back in my bedroom, I did the whole young scientist routine, dipping an eye dropper of my mum's into the pail and depositing a sample on to a slide. One look at the wriggling sci-fi creatures that inhabited the brook in their billions was enough to put you off paddling there for good.

Card collecting has always been a part of childhood. I'm not old enough to recall the glory years of cigarette cards, my intro to it coming from Brooke Bond tea packets. I'd just missed the Wild Flowers series, but by the time Freshwater Fish started I was all keyed up for the chase. I should feel shame when I admit to this, seeing how much I tutted and grumbled when my own children were fascinated by Pokémon cards. Like them, I became obsessed with completing a set of Chubb, Perch, Barbel and so on. Mind you, at least the tea cards were free, rather than costing over two pounds for a pack of eleven! And I can honestly say that they were of sound educational value.

But some aspects of our respective collecting were identical, such as impatience. No sooner had a new packet of tea entered the house than it was violated. Mum would be furious when she went to the cupboard and found packets with their outer side already ripped off where I'd dived in to get at the cards. Usually you could tell on which side of the packet the card was inserted, but if you made a wrong guess it meant ripping off another side, too. Worst-case scenario was having to rip off all four sides, leaving the inner bag surrounded by tatters of green paper. Then I got smart and hit upon the idea of using Mum's tweezers. Folding back the top of the pack, it was possible to slide the tweezers down the side to grab the card. You had to have the talents of a bomb-disposal expert – misjudge it and the sharp corner of the tweezers could rip the bag, leaving a hole which dispensed a thin trickle of tea leaves.

A year or two earlier, encouraged by Mum, I'd started to collect History of the Wild West cards from packs of Weetabix. My mum, as good mothers will, sent off for the album, and when it arrived I dutifully began to stick in the cards. The smell of Bostik still brings it all back to me, sitting on the carpet in front of the fire with my snippets of life in the Wild West. And very instructive they were, too, with card titles such as 'Rifles that Conquered the West', 'Dress of Seminole', 'Iroquois Indians', 'Hunting the Buffalo', 'Trails to the West' and 'The Wells Fargo Stagecoach'. But, hey, what's this – titter, snigger? Card No.18 – 'A Sod House on the Prairie'. I'd only ever come across 'sod' as a swear word so I was deeply puzzled with this part of my collection – and not a little guilty!

Of course, card collecting had (still does have) a very strong social angle. At junior and secondary school the swapping and trading of cards was undertaken every bit as seriously as working the floor of the Stock Exchange. Additions to a collection could always be won, too, by the time-honoured game of skimming them up against a wall to see whose got closest – winner takes all. There were cards representing every conceivable aspect of life past and present – from the educational Kings and Queens of England to the soon-to-be ubiquitous football cards featuring just about every player from the First Division.

They say if a billion butterflies moved their wings at once the Earth could be shifted from its orbit. So it's surprising that our modest little planet wasn't well on the way to the asteroid belt with all the tens of millions of children who used to shake their cereal packets in an effort to see where the free gift was. Dredged to the surface, inched up by a variety of tactics, once the cereal dust and sugar was blown off it, the cereal-box toy was a genuinely prized item – if only for a day or two. There were dozens of free toys around, most of them inspired by TV programmes. Kellogg's were the most generous, and their Corn Flakes, Frosties and Rice Krispies had all sorts of figures, from a set of traditional Robin Hood figures (the amount of plastic in Friar Tuck would have been enough to knock out a cat!), *Magic Roundabout* characters and and a set of six from *Thunderbirds*. But the most fondly remembered was a deep-sea diver – based, I guess, on the hero of a programme called *Sea Hunt*. It was more than a simple plastic figure: the idea was to put a tiny amount of baking powder in the figure, then drop it through the neck of a pop bottle filled with water. The diver dropped to the bottom in fine underwater style, then after a minute or so made an authentic ascent to the surface. Magic!

You could even get a gun from the back of Corn Flakes boxes. After first cutting out the two halves along the dotted lines, you had to score and fold them carefully. The two halves were then secured with a paperclip and elastic band. Of course, it wasn't as satisfying as a die-cast cap-firing gun – and was especially useless in the rain – but so long as you had something to point at enemies you'd be entitled to join in the latest session of Cowboys and Indians down at the dump. On reflection, I think they were intended to be educational rather than practical. Why else was I the only one to be fighting my corner of the Wild West expansionist dream with an eighteenth-century flintlock? It's remarkable that no one ever noticed.

My first and only wigwam came courtesy of Weetabix. No, it wasn't carefully folded into the box – that would have been asking a bit too much – but my mum filled in a coupon and sent if off with a seven and six postal order and the obligatory pack tops. I loved it: it was red and yellow fabric with three sectional poles. We set it up on the lawn and I sat in it...and sat in it...and sat in it. It was too small to do much else but sit in it, and there was certainly no room to stretch out and make papooses, even if I'd been anywhere near the age of consent. So I just sat cross-legged at the entrance and tried to look important, like a chief.

The Viewmaster counts as a major part of my childhood toy sequence. An updated version of the Victorian stereoscope in sturdy Bakelite/brown plastic, the Viewmaster first made its appearance in the 1930s, introduced by the Sawyer Company. The pictures were provided – and this was the innovation – not in twosomes mounted on a card but on a revolving disc which was slotted in the top of the device. They were then turned one picture at a time by a lever at the side. Viewmasters were all the rage, for one year. I'm not sure if Mum bought it for her own edification, but I'd soon co-opted it. The biggest drawback, if indeed it was, was that virtually all the discs were on American themes – 'Tour of the Rockies', 'Views of New York', and so on – with no deference to anything British save an American tourist's intro to London Town – Tower Bridge, Westminster Abbey, Chelsea Pensioners – and one bizarre 'action' set featuring unemployed actors playing out the story of Robin Hood, in glorious 3-D. But the early sixties marked the zenith of our 'special relationship', so the American slant wasn't resented; quite the opposite, it counted as Stateside glamour and it would have been almost treacherous to complain. If Yanks loved the Grand Canyon who were we to gainsay their opinions?

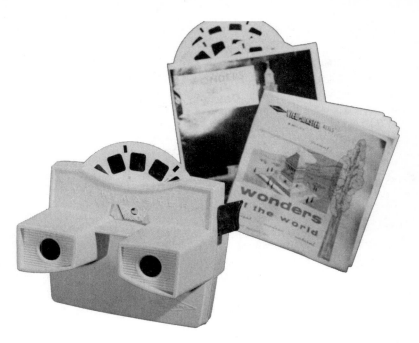

The 1960s Viewmaster and slides (Hulton Getty)

'Bottle of meths please.'

With all today's wariness about the misuse of glue and lighter fuel, it's hard to imagine any twenty-first-century chemist catering to such a request from a fourteen-year-old boy. Not if he wanted to stay out of the papers or keep his membership of the Pharmaceutical Association. In the mid-sixties, though, the rules were obviously more relaxed and I was a glutton for the purple stuff. There was a time when I couldn't get enough, even though financial constraints forced down my consumption to one bottle a week. In the 1960s chemists, like opticians, were more interesting folk, their shelves graced by all manner of obscure potions and powders. Try going into Boots now and asking for methylated spirits: the squeaky-clean shop assistants probably wouldn't even know what it is.

My request was perfectly innocent. The meths wasn't for

drinking, or even for laying down. No, it was essential fuel for my latest toy, the Mamod Steam Engine.

The Mamod range belonged firmly to the *Boy's Own* world: models of real steam engines in gleaming brass and burnished steel. A Mamod provided an education in all kinds of engineering basics – steam power, pistons, safety-valves. There were more expensive mobile versions available – like a steamroller – but my static version was fascinating enough. Riveted to a sturdy metal base, it had smoothly engineered pistons, safety-valve, whistle and flywheel. The chimney was really just ornamental, but it looked good.

The Mamod needed some patience. After first funnelling a half-pint of water into the boiler (plastic funnel provided) you moved to the heating stage. Heat was provided from a rectangular tray stuffed with cotton-wool and enclosed by a grilled plate. You soaked the wool with the meths, struck a match and off you went. A steady hand was essential: any spillage on the engine or even on your hands was liable to ignite, sometimes with alarming results. Seeing your hand catch fire could induce understandable panic, but I quickly realised that the heat wasn't ferocious and began to do it just for fun, panicking old ladies by rushing out into the street with my hand alight and feigning disaster.

The heating power was rather low key and you could boil three or four kettles for your teapot before there was any response from the Mamod's boiler. But it was well worth the wait. Those first soft jerks of movement were as beautiful as a new-born foal trying out its legs. Sometimes the engine needed a nudge or two, but once it got going full steam ahead the sight was brilliant. The precision engineering took your breath away and all you could do was admire it, because that was really all there was to do. Mamod also provided several accessories like a steam hammer and a sewing-machine that were, supposedly, able to run off the stationary steam engine, but I could never get them to work. Maybe I didn't have the right connections: the parcel string my mum provided just didn't have the same tension or grip provided by the official rubberised band.

My childhood was always tinged with one regret: that I

never had a model railway. Not a proper one at least. When I was about eight or nine I was invited into another boy's garden shed to see the model railway his dad had built for him. 'Hornby-Dublo, Hornby-Dublo,' he kept twittering excitedly. His mantra may as well have been a brand of Hungarian washing powder for all it meant to me, but once inside the shed I became immediately entranced. There, lovingly constructed on a proper baseboard, was a fantastic model railway, a working world in miniature. It had gleaming track, engines, trucks and little white posts with red-and-yellow signal arms. There was an intoxicating fragrance of electricity and oil. This fascinating miniature world needed a god – and here he was, at the controls of a grey galvanised transformer with chunky knobs. I wasn't allowed anywhere near the transformer – that was the host's prerogative – but I was content for the moment to watch and envy.

Things weren't 100 per cent automatic: it was still necessary to do your own level-crossing opening and tip up the signal arms with a finger – and I was thrilled to be the guest signalman. Your imagination could enjoy free rein. The realistic-looking ballast on which the track was laid was merely crushed birdseed sprayed with grey paint.

I hadn't yet started trainspotting, so the appeal of trains was a hazy concept, but after being allowed to feel the weight of a Coronation loco in my hands I knew I had to have a layout of my own. But there was a big but. To have a decent kind of model railway you needed either a garden shed or a house with an attic or a spare room. My best friend at grammar school had a detached garage with a loft, a huge space which was ideal for a model railway. Unfortunately, my family had neither garage or loft and our garden shed was just big enough for a wheelbarrow and some tools.

For years I just dreamed, picking up each new Hornby-Dublo catalogue as it came out and quietly planning. During lessons at school I drew fantastic layouts that would have required a ballroom and a hundred pounds' worth of track just to get started! In the end, determined not to be excluded from the model-railway brotherhood, in the lead up to Christmas 1968, I turned on the emotional screws and got my mum to buy me a basic Triang-Hornby set. Anticipating it, I'd even risked buying a second-hand Jinty 0–6–0, bought with my pocket money from a classmate. With my two engines, two coaches and three trucks I began to set up business on my bedroom floor. But permanence was impossible when my mum insisted on hoovering every Saturday, and I didn't really know what I was doing, either. Defiantly I glued my track down to some hardboard, but instantly regretted not being able to change the set-up.

I had a fascination, applicable to all toys, of the miniature. It's all about feeling a thousand times bigger than the toy you're controlling, whether it's a doll, a car or a whole rural railway station. You are God, benevolent or otherwise. It's your choice. Toys teach us we have power, but they give us the opportunity to choose how we use that power. Girls learn to be nurturing mother figures, boys indulge themselves as angry gods, hurling lorries and ships to an awful doom, arranging spectacular crashes which never do the toys much good. Needless cruelty was part of it, too, for I still feel guilty even now for putting my pet white mouse on the back of a coal truck and sending him on a dizzying journey round and round.

I can't remember what my last toy was and when my Christmases became all LPs, books or even – horrors! – socks, pants and talcum powder. But it happens to us all – mums and dads and all those kindly aunts and uncles just stop buying you toys. There is a time for everyone when Christmas isn't the same and there are no stockings or sacks to dive into. The last sugar pig has gone unrecorded and who can recall the fate of that last stocking, and whether it was returned to its intended function as footwear?

But is there ever a 'last toy' or is it just a matter of semantics. Really, isn't my latest hi-fi or mobile phone just another toy?

The end of the 1960s marked the end of my childhood, age-wise and place-wise. I'd been lucky enough to grow up next to green fields and clear streams. I'd spent my days going from one novelty to another: from sticking Weetabix and Brooke Bond cards into their albums to paddling in the brook with my fishing-net to sitting in my wigwam or doing early morning checks on my weather station equipment. But it was time to leave. In my bedroom I had a huge tin trunk overflowing with toy wreckage. It was all here, dislocated, disassembled, broken: Bayko rods and brickwork, toy cowboys and soldiers, wheels and axles, coloured pegs from obscure games, counters and discoloured dice, a hundred jigsaw puzzle pieces that even a million monkeys with a million years could never turn into a picture. This was my childhood of toys, like flotsam washed up on a beach. I didn't want to let go. Even now I can visualise some of those individual jigsaw puzzle pieces: a section of ship's rigging, a corner of a castle, the eye of a cute spaniel. But we couldn't take it with us and, anyway, I didn't feel I wanted to. By then I was too into the Rolling Stones and Marmalade and learning to play a wonky guitar to have time for childish things. It was just a tin box of rubbish that no one could be bothered to dump. But dump it we did, without much sentiment, tipping the toys into the bin and arranging for the council to come and collect the heavy trunk itself.

That's childhood for you: so unprecious at the time, so taken for granted and easily discarded. But now I've come to realise there are grown men out there – responsible bankers, managers and salesmen – who would have paid good money for the privilege of snouting through that trunk. Grown men just like me who get a weird thrill at the smell of a tyre from a Corgi car or the touch of a clammy plastic cowboy with bandy legs.

1970s and 1980s

Sindy, the bestselling toy of 1970, was a natural choice for the British market. True, she was little more than a copy of the American prototype, Barbie, but wise heads in the toy industry must have realised that the idea wasn't wholly transferable to the UK market. Barbie was unmistakably American, unmistakably plasticky – literally and figuratively. Though it was never intentional, Barbie's doll-like appearance was destined to become a style goal for millions of American women. By default, the plastic look became an authentic fashion statement.

Even the name wasn't right for the British market. Nobody in Britain ever shortened the name Barbara to Barbie. Babs was much more cuddly, just like everyone's favourite busty blonde from the *Carry On* films. Barbie sounded like a man-eater. Sindy was much more in tune with the British character: certainly girly but somehow old-fashioned and distinctly non-sexy.

Anyway, we liked our dolls with brains. Not for us the vacuous transatlantic platinum blonde. Keeping Sindy company was Katy Copycat, the writing doll. OK, her writing may have been more of the secretarial variety than anything Brontë-esque, but it showed that British girls had higher aspirations for their make-believe offspring than simply getting them into the Miss Bimbo 1971 Contest.

Cerebral pastimes were the order of the day and with 1973 proving to be the height of *Mastermind* mania it was no surprise that the year's bestseller in the toyshops was a board game inspired by the TV programme. For one glorious year, Magnus Magnusson was not just the world's most famous Icelander but also an unlikely role-model for girls and boys. There'd been

Sindy (and her 'boyfriend' Paul) model late-sixties ski wear (Hulton Getty)

board games based on TV shows before – *Take Your Pick*, *Double Your Money* – but their hosts were old-school showbiz types, far too jolly to be cool. The *Mastermind* format, with its black chair and austere quizmaster, was only just the right side of sadism! Though it became the craze of 1973 and 1974, the board game was very much in the old tradition of pitting wits and general knowledge against a family-appointed quizmaster, foreshadowing yuppie favourite *Trivial Pursuit* in the eighties and the more populist *Who Wants to Be a Millionaire*, which was destined to be the top-selling game during the last Christmas season of the twentieth century.

But while the traditions of the past still had their place, the 1970s was really the start of a whole new genre of toys – made possible through the march of technology. I was on holiday in Paignton in September 1976 when I first came across Pong. In one of the amusement arcades by the railway station the prototype video game was the star attraction. It was a time when one-armed bandits and pinball were still the mainstay in the nation's arcades and you could see that many of the older holidaymakers regarded this video novelty with suspicion. To be honest, if it had been noisy and flash and complicated, like the soon-to-arrive Space Invaders, I probably wouldn't have bothered – and my mum certainly wouldn't! But the table-tennis that Pong was based on was a game that everyone, young and old, knew how to play. Pong was a winner. The name was daft, the bleeps a novelty, and the ups and downs of playing it had a slapstick quality that kept us laughing all week. Since the school holidays had finished there was no competition from the crowds of juveniles who'd been hogging it all through the summer...

Pong was invented by Nolan Bushnell, and proved such a worldwide winner that it provided him with the money to set up video pioneers Atari. As a child in 1940s Utah, Bushnell had a childhood typical of a would-be inventor. He was a star pupil in science classes, though legend has it that he nearly burned down the family garage with a homemade rocket mounted on a roller-skate! When his father died, Bushnell took over the family concrete business and soon proved that he possessed a shrewd business brain. His destiny came into focus during his time at the University of Utah studying computer graphics. Intrigued by the potential of combining the new computer possibilities with family amusements, he invented his first video game, Computer Space, in 1970. Looking very much like a prototype of the later Asteroids, Computer Space proved too complicated and cumbersome for mass production.

Undeterred, Bushnell devised the much simpler Pong, a video version of ping-pong whose 'ball' was a white blip that bounced back and forth across the screen between two 'bats' that were moved up and down by control knobs. The new game had a trial run in a Californian bar during 1971. It proved a victim of its own success, being so overplayed and stuffed with coins that it eventually broke down.

Knowing he had a winning product, Bushnell recruited a friend and founded Atari in 1972, with just five hundred dollars. The company's games over the next few years – including Asteroids – gave rise not only to the video arcade, but to an entire industry. It is safe to say that Bushnell and Atari changed the landscape of amusements for ever.

A home version of Pong arrived in 1975. Plugged into the aerial socket of the family TV, it was an even greater milestone, marking a time when TV sets offered a simple alternative to adverts and soap operas and people could enjoy all the excitement of an arcade in their own living room.

Other companies were quick to invest in the video-game business, and before long just about every sports activity – from hockey and tennis to snooker and squash – was available in two-dimensional format, so that even the laziest couch potatoes could feel that they were being active!

By the time my mum and I were getting into Pong, Bushnell had sold Atari to Time-Warner for $28 million. By 1982, Atari was bringing in about £3 billion a year.

But even video empires decline and fall... The future was promised to the Japanese computer-game giants Sony and Nintendo.

Science-fiction toys had enjoyed two peaks with Dan Dare merchandise in the late 1950s and Dr Who in the mid-1960s. Amazing as it was scientifically, the Apollo moon programme never really did much to inspire children's games. Neil Armstrong may have been the greatest explorer of the twentieth century, but he wasn't the kind of hero you could build a shootout game around! Still, the toy and model shops did a steady trade with the various Airfix kits based on the Apollo programme, and a plastic mini-version of the Eagle lunar module had pride of place in many a home.

By the mid-1970s, though, space-race fever had rather faded in the public consciousness. We looked at the moon, thought, 'Been there, done that,' and shrugged. Until *Star Wars* hit the cinemas in 1977. Then we were in for a space-toy boom that had known no equal. The toyshops were invaded by all manner of weird and wonderful figures – Luke Skywalker, Darth Vader, R2D2, C3PO and a whole galactic soap opera's cast of characters. Forget plastic swords, there weren't many kids who didn't aspire to the latest in weaponry: the light sabre. The fact that it looked suspiciously like a fluorescent strip light was neither here nor there... that's what imagination's for.

Star Wars products were hardly the first toys to tie-in with a film, but merchandising had never been so comprehensive.

Everywhere you looked – for a few months at least – all the little girls were doing each other's hair like Princess Leia's. The marketing venture had been cranked up to a phenomenal pitch, with billions of dollars at stake.

Even Lego cashed in on the revived craze for space. Unbeatable favourite throughout the seventies, Lego topped the bestselling toy charts in 1974 and 1975, but simple bricks weren't enough and with the Lego Space Kit, brought out in 1979, they again managed to pull off the coup of having the year's bestselling toy. Though there were plenty of challengers, it was unlikely that any construction toy would now dislodge Lego from its pre-eminent place in the hearts and minds of children.

Another old favourite – and this one was British! – was also still around, and was improving all the time. Subbuteo's cardboard players were substituted in 1967 for celluloid versions that were described as 'scientifically designed to be 100 per cent self-balancing and almost unbreakable'. Generic sets were no longer good enough for the increasing army of Subbuteo fans, who would only play with the real thing. Fifty team strips were available, along with a range of accessories, such as a miniature referee's whistle and an automatic timekeeper.

The familiar 3-D figures that followed had first been mooted in the late 1950s. Originally dubbed 'Continental Type', the hand-painted figures were designed by Charles Stadden, an experienced military modeller who was also responsible for the figures in Scalextric cars. Players demanded ever more realism to make their games look better and new accessories included floodlights, a red perimeter fence with advertising boards, training kits, a manager, trainer and photographers. There was even a short-lived Subbuteo tie, a badly judged example of taking brand loyalty a little too far.

It was inevitable that Subbuteo would diversify by trying to market the same thing with cricket and rugby. Though both of these games proved less easy to play than football, they were moderately successful and by the 1970s there were twenty-six different rugby-team strips. The cricket, played on a large green-baize oval, featured a bowler figure which was simply one of the early two-dimensional footballers, with a picture of a bowler affixed, his arm raised where the footballer's head had been. At the rear of the base was a wire triangle into which the ball (much smaller than the football in soccer Subbuteo, and red, of course) was placed. A flick on the back of the bowler sent the ball towards the wicket in 'genuine overarm bowling motion'. The wire triangle could even be tilted left or right to impart off-spin or leg-spin! In addition to the usable scoreboard, there were several spectators, one of whom was accurately posed asleep in his deckchair.

Shorter-lived spin-offs included Snooker Express, a game played by flicking a player at the balls *à la* Subbuteo. Targetman, meanwhile, was aimed at younger soccer fans. Older players would scorn it as a little too gimmicky: the right leg of each Targetman player had a spring clip, enabling it to be pulled back and let go to strike the ball. There was even Subbuteo Angling, though this was more of a traditional board game. Players moved around the board collecting tackle, bait and suchlike until they had all the necessary equipment needed for a fishing trip. Once a place to fish had been won, the players stated the kind of fish they were fishing for. A 'ready reckoner' was provided to calculate the weight and the biggest fish won. The key component of Subbuteo Angling was a strange UFO-shaped device into which a dried pea was dropped. This was used in place of dice. Subbuteo Hockey, and Sport Billy – described as Subbuteo for youngsters – followed. Sport Billy was the first indication of modern marketing techniques. Billy, used as a mascot at one World Cup, was a European cartoon character who represented 'fair play in sport'.

The 1970s witnessed the first Subbuteo World Cup – known as the John Waddington World Cup Trophy in honour of the games company who had taken over Subbuteo production. There followed a significant increase in the club colours available – 165 of them by 1973 – and it looked as if Subbuteo football had become almost as popular as the game itself. The

Daily Express even sponsored five-a-side Subbuteo tournaments, which were played on the Wednesday night TV programme *Sportsnight*.

Subbuteo mania demanded ever grander concepts and there were expensive sets such as the Munich World Series, and the Stadium Edition which included a large grandstand. For the truly dedicated there was even a 45 r.p.m. disc to buy – 'The Subbuteo Sound' – a record of the Subbuteo World Cup song. The 1981 range featured a *World of Sport* set containing the football Stadium Edition, plus full rugby and cricket sets in a huge carrying case. It cost seventy-five pounds and only a thousand were ever made.

Players were redesigned again (for the last time) to a figure which both combined and improved upon the two previous designs. Figures from this point on were machine painted, and although this sometimes resulted in white lines under the arms, it allowed for badges and shirt advertising and any manner of strange kit to be reproduced. Starting with the 1982 World Cup, boxes were redesigned to display the whole team. New accessories reflected the modern state of football, with a high crowd barrier, mounted police, crush barriers and even a rubber-backed astropitch. The fast-moving pace of shirt changes finally forced Subbuteo to remove out-of-date kits from its product range. By the end of the 1980s football teams were changing kits every year and having two away strips. Subbuteo heroically strove to keep up. One change that hit the headlines was the standard addition of three black players to each team to reflect the ethnic diversity of the English leagues.

Other British institutions weren't having the success enjoyed by Subbuteo. Mattel's Hot Wheels had had a serious effect on the sales of Britain's Matchbox toys at the end of the sixties. The British company did not take this lying down, though, and fought back with its own 'Superfast' range of cars. During 1970 and 1971 the entire Matchbox range was converted to the Superfast wheels. In 1973, Matchbox's die-casting genius, Jack O'Dell, resigned from the company, leaving Leslie Smith as sole director. The same year saw many new additions to the

Matchbox range, including 'Rolomatics', which featured parts that moved as the wheels revolved. But the company was beset by troubles of an almost biblical nature. After a crippling eight-week strike by production workers, the company was hit in quick succession by a fire and a flood. A boardroom decision was made to diversify, and Lesney acquired the Vogue Doll Company and a manufacturer of plastic model kits. Despite a potentially profitable franchise to make Disney figures, manufacturing in the Far East proved too much of a financial burden, and after suffering huge losses the famous Lesney firm was finally declared bankrupt in 1992.

The skateboard, another American import, can be traced back to the early 1900s, when kids first had the idea of fixing roller-skate wheels to a board. The board would often have some kind of box attached for the driver to sit in – very much like the English trolley. Always on the lookout for new thrills, over the decades kids changed the look by removing the crate and balancing themselves on the board itself. Over the years people began to take it more seriously, making modifications to the trucks (the device that holds the wheels) so that the prototype 'skateboards' acquired much greater manoeuvrability.

With the increased popularity of surfing during the 1950s it wasn't long before someone came up with the idea of combining the two thrills. 'Sidewalk surfing' began to catch on among the surf crowd, but it wasn't until the magazine *Surf Guide* began to advertise properly made skateboards that things really took off. The first professional boards were made in 1963 and champion surfer Hobie Alter created Hobie Skateboards. With international contests, movies like *Skater Dater* and a magazine, *The Quarterly Skateboarder*, the pastime became a craze. Over fifty million skateboards were sold within a three-year period.

The first reversal came in the late sixties. Manufacturers were so busy making the boards that little time was spent on research. Although better wheels were available, clay ones were cheaper, but as they lacked good grip, skateboarding accidents were common – and some were fatal. There was a public back-lash against the plague of skateboarders on the streets. In response, many American cities banned them and manufacturers lost enormous amounts of money due to cancelled orders.

In the following years skateboarding went underground. Away from the streets, die-hard skateboarders had plenty of time and space to develop and experiment. In an effort to repopularise their sport they developed the kicktail and other tricks, but they met with only limited success.

The revival and subsequent worldwide craze of the seventies was due to a technical advance. In 1970 surfer Frank Nasworthy started to develop a board with urethane wheels which gave much greater traction and hence better control. He began to promote the new skateboard in the San Diego area and after initial resistance the new wheels gained a following. Word spread. The so-called 'Cadillac Wheels' gave skateboarding a second lease of life and during the early 1970s board manufacturers came up with a host of improvements and new ideas. Skateboards were made two or three inches wider to give better stability on vertical surfaces. With these new easy-riding boards, slalom, downhill and freestyle skateboarding began to be practised by millions. *SkateBoarder* magazine was resurrected and joined by others hoping to cash in. In 1976 the first purpose-built skateboarding park was opened in Florida and was soon followed by hundreds all over the USA. Fashion also became part of the skateboarding experience, starting with decorated boards, a trend that was followed by almost all board manufacturers. The new generation of skateboarders began to mesh with punk and new wave music devotees.

But the sport was getting too popular for its own good. Due to the vast numbers of visitors, insurance for skateboarding parks became exorbitantly expensive – so much so that many owners were forced to close their doors. By the end of 1980, skateboarding was in recession yet again.

As BMX became popular and *SkateBoarder* magazine diversified many skateboarders deserted and those that kept the faith moved underground once more. A hardcore contingent were forced to build half-pipes and ramps in their backyards and on patches of wasteground as the skateparks closed for good.

Although skateboarding contests were held, the turnout was small and the prize money even smaller. By 1984, skateboarders were only interested in streetstyle skating and launch ramps. The first 'Bones Brigade' videos were released – helping to propel skateboarding to new levels of popularity. The focus was on ollies and other technical tricks rather than the half-pipes of the seventies. Royalties and contest winnings escalated and with contests throughout the world some pro skaters earned as much as two thousand dollars a week. Skateboard fashion became enormously popular.

By 1991, the worldwide recession had hit the skateboard industry hard. It managed a third renaissance in the mid-1990s, when it was rebranded as an 'extreme sport'. Towards the end of the nineties, skateboarding's focus remained on streetstyle and fashion with top skateboarders invariably setting up their own companies to sell clothes and boards. As with the surfing counter-culture from which it developed, skateboarding always managed to keep the big companies and marketing men at a safe distance.

If Ideal Toys' marketing men had been stuck on the original name – Buvuos Kocka – it may never have become a hit. If its inventor had been christened Smith, it would have forever lacked those faintly nutty Ruritanian overtones that caught our attention. But they weren't and he wasn't. As Rubik's Cube this mind-boggling plaything was destined to become one of the biggest leisure-time obsessions of Thatcher's eighties – a geometric rosary for the yuppie years.

Erno Rubik, a Hungarian mathematician, had been fascinated by the idea for some time. His initial aim had not been to invent a toy, but simply to solve a structural design problem that had been bugging him. He'd made a cube consisting of fifty-four individual smaller cubes – called 'cubies' – and set himself the problem of how to move the cubies independently without the main cube falling apart.

Invented by Erno Rubik, a Hungarian mathematician (Robert Opie Collection)

After a succession of failed prototypes, some held together only with elastic bands and enthusiasm, Rubik came up with the solution which every exasperated player who ripped the thing apart will know. After hand-carving individual cubies and slotting them together to make up the big cube, he marked each of the faces with adhesive paper of a different colour. Then he began twisting. As each cubie took with it the colour from its 'home' face Rubik hoped to track the movements. In just half a dozen twists utter confusion reigned. As Rubik himself put it, 'It was at that moment that I came face to face with the Big Challenge: What is the way home?'

An American, Larry Nichols, had already patented a similar cube held together with magnets, but his toy was rejected by all the big toy companies, including Ideal Toys, who bought the rights to Rubik's Cube.

With his intended name – Magic Cube – already registered to another device, trademark laws forced Rubik to look for an alternative. After racking his brains and failing to come up with anything particularly snappy, he settled on his own name.

In the best traditions of Communist Eastern Europe, the first Rubik's Cubes were put together by a toy-making co-operative in Budapest. Maybe the authorities thought that Warsaw Pact kiddies would get so obsessed with cubing they'd forget about the exciting *Star Wars* toys that children across in the decadent West were playing with. But sales of Rubik's Cube were sluggish until it was discovered by a Hungarian entre-preneur on the lookout for new schemes. Sitting in a Budapest café, Tibor Laczi was fascinated as he watched while a waiter played with one of the cubes. He rushed off to buy one for himself, and even though he couldn't solve it himself he knew straight away it could be a winner. After receiving permission from the Hungarian state trading company Konsumex to try to sell the Cube in the West, Laczi arranged a meeting with its inventor.

'When Rubik first walked into the room I felt like giving him some money,' Laczi said. 'He was terribly dressed, and had a cheap Hungarian cigarette hanging out of his mouth. But I knew I had a genius on my hands. I told him we could sell millions.'

Though not booked in as an official exhibitor, Laczi went off to the next Nuremberg Toy Fair. Without a stall of his own from which to tout for business, he attracted attention by simply walking around playing with the Cube. One man on whom he made an impression was British toy expert Tom Kremer. He couldn't help but agree that the toy had great potential. Using his influence, he persuaded Ideal Toys to place an order for a million Cubes, setting in train a worldwide mania that would make Erno Rubik a millionaire.

Rubik had invented a toy that transcended ideology and national borders. Though it may have started off as a cheap amusement for impoverished Iron Curtain folk, it came to exert such a fascination on the West that it was the bestselling toy in 1980. People everywhere, young and old, were twisting, thumbing and rotating their way to nervous exhaustion. For some it all proved too much: tempers frayed, people yelled at each other, some even smashed household items. Today the media would probably dub it 'Cube rage'.

While anyone over twenty gained nothing more than heightened blood pressure and a few grey hairs from the Cubes, they were constantly reminded of their inadequacy. A steady stream of prodigies popped up on our TV screens: viewers were presented with remarkable sprogs who could pick up a Rubik's Cube and complete it in well under a minute. A sixteen-year-old Vietnamese high-school student from LA, Minh Thai, won the world championship in Budapest by unscrambling a Cube in 22.95 seconds. Determined not to be outdone by these dexterous show-offs, we carried on buying enough of them to make it the bestselling toy of 1981, too.

Handbooks appeared by the dozen, several of which became bestsellers in their own rights. But even the books were a headache. Others soon devised their own clever solutions. After carefully disassembling the Cube and putting it back together, you could rush into the office shrieking, 'I've done it, I've done it,' and brazenly take all the pats on the back and looks of envy. Until they asked you to do it again in front of witnesses...Another trick was simply to peel off the coloured squares and stick them all back in an ordered fashion.

But after a couple of years of headaches, guilt, envy and frustration most of us had had enough. Those of us who managed it – as I did eventually – showed off our brilliance to a few friends and that was it. Once everyone had had a go, the Rubik's Cube was fated to become one of history's more amusing quirks. Toyshops tried to get us going again with variations such as the Rubik's Snake, but it had neither the novelty value to interest us nor, indeed, the Cube's colourful iconic appearance.

My Little Pony first cantered on to the scene as the Cube was starting to wane in 1981. Made of hard plastic and ten inches tall, these bizarrely styled equines were originally sold as My Pretty Pony. Each one had a trigger underneath its chin, a pull on which would cause the pony to flick its ears, twitch its tail and – more alarmingly – wink. The first vinyl-based mutations of the species appeared the following year, in a set of six, saddled with names even more startling than their colouring: Cotton Candy, Snuzzle, Blossom and Minty.

But these weren't just any old ponies. Unlike Tishy – the 1920s cuddly pony who trotted off some anonymous production line – MLPs hailed from a magic country called Ponyland, with cities such as Dream Valley, Friendship Gardens and Vulcanopolis, the last of these established as a retreat for ponies who had fled from the doomed Atlantis. Calculating toymakers knew that background stories like these stimulated children's interest. Take a basic product, issue it in a dozen or so variations and collecting becomes almost an obsession for the child...and an ongoing moneyspinner for the manufacturer. These refugee ponies needed caring for and every little girl wanted the job. TV adverts showed the ponies having their psychedelically coloured manes groomed. It seemed that no little girl's bedroom was complete without at least one example of the species...and preferably the whole set.

Hasbro continued making My Little Pony for ten years, but

the last one reared its pretty little head in 1991. Their demise was perhaps hastened by an overdose of cuteness brought about by names of ever-increasing sweetness: Sweet Kisses, Colorswirl, Sundazzle, Flower Fantasy and Paradise Baby. Even within a ten-year span people had noticed that girls seemed to be getting streetwise at an increasingly young age and 'days of innocence' – like some of the toys – were beginning to have an all too limited run. The age group that had originally taken My Little Pony to its heart in 1981 was now just as likely to be into make-up, Australian soaps and boy bands of a beastly background.

I was working as an advertising copywriter when I first came across some more eighties cuties, the Sylvanian Family. Not being a parent, I was unaware that for a remarkable three years – in 1987, 1988 and 1989 – the Sylvanian Family had taken the honours as Britain's bestselling toy. Subconsciously I always added a prefix 'trans' whenever I thought of them, imagining a set of figures based on a kind of European Addams Family set up. When the truth was finally revealed – someone tipped a box of them on to my desk with instructions to make the nation's catalogue browsers love them – I couldn't help feeling guilty. How could I have slandered these cute little woodland creatures? No bloody fangs or neck bolts here, no bat wings or deathly complexions, just a bundle of bunnies looking for love and good PR.

But we media manipulators weren't having it all our own way. The 1980s brought increased wariness from consumers and protective parents. With various watchdog programmes on TV, there was a new assertiveness about safety and design issues and a heightened desire to protect children from danger. There'd always been scares: in the fifties the British were scathing about the quality of any product sporting a 'Made in Hong Kong' label and horror stories about flammable Teddies and dolls containing shards of stiletto-sharp steel were legion.

TV's plethora of consumer-protection programmes featured toys – from dangerous playground equipment to cutesy dolls – with monotonous regularity. Consumer champions submitted toys and dolls to shocking autopsies: eyes were yanked out, heads snapped off, limbs twisted, textile guts removed. TV viewers were shown cuddly dolls becoming fireballs when exposed to a flame. Pictures of the £6.99 Rainbow Clone – made in Taiwan – revealed a distressing scene of a doll that looked like the victim of spontaneous combustion. As if that wasn't enough, anyone who pulled off the doll's nose would expose a three-centimetre spike.

Perhaps as a result of these horrors there was a move back to old standards, with a revival of solid wooden toys. No doubt there was an element of nostalgia mixed up in it, too.

The eighties were certainly a decade of contrast. On the one hand, the microchip was making its presence felt. Scamp – acronym for the Self-Contained Autonomous Mobile with Personality – was a sixteen–inch–high fluffy puppy that came complete with 300 different whines, bleeps and grunts to signify its feelings. Thanks to the wonders of silicon science the Scamps could be made so that no two were identical. According to the publicity, it was the first toy to have real emotions – a range of twelve distinct moods which included affection, boredom, contentment, fear and sadness. It even snarled when irritated. Scamp's behaviour encompassed a set of probable behaviour patterns, but random programming of his microchips ensured that nothing happened with any certainty. What the makers failed to realise was that real puppies are utterly predictable – guaranteed to jump on to your lap when you have a cup of hot tea...

But if Scamp was at the cutting edge, a much more successful toy was a throwback (or certainly looked like one). Cabbage Patch Kids were the bestselling toys of 1984.

The lumpen dolls were invented by one Xavier 'Happy' Roberts in the 1970s to help pay his way through art school. Relaunched a decade on, the marketing brains hit on a clever ruse: the forlorn-looking dolls would not be offered for sale, but for adoption. Each one came with its own birth certificate and millions were 'adopted' during 1983 and 1984, making Cabbage Patch Kids the most successful dolls in the history of the toy industry.

Demand was stoked up by a host of media stories, pre-packaged urban myths about the depths that shoppers would go to in their buying frenzy. Parents were going crazy in their rush to get hold of the dolls while shop-owners were accused of many devious practices, such as reserving dolls for influential customers, selling them to the highest bidders, or even stock-piling them as some kind of cynical investment portfolio. The newspapers brainwashed parents as effectively as any religious cult: other parents were your enemy; they wanted to spoil your children's Christmas; they wanted to laugh at you as they rushed away from the toyshop with the very last Cabbage Patch Kid. Some trod on your toes, others elbowed you in the ribs, and some weren't above lashing out with a right hook if it meant taking a prized Cabbage Patch Kid home to the family. The message was clear: win that fight; get that doll; impress your children; taste victory.

If George Orwell had been granted a chance to revise *1984*, maybe he'd have devised a more fitting and contemporary punishment for Winston Smith. For instance, why not make him a parent anxiously tracking down a Cabbage Patch Kid for a spoiled offspring? Why not make Room 101 an empty toyshop, its shelves devoid of Cabbage Patch Kids. The punishment is then to leave Room 101 and go home to tell the child the news...It would have been a far more harrowing experience than any monkey business with rodents.

The unfathomable early eighties craze for the 'lumpen' Cabbage Patch Dolls set the tone for chaos at Christmas in recent times (Robert Opie Collection)

Cabbage Patch fever raged for some three years but eventually subsided. Plainness was no longer cute. Nevertheless, in its best years the Cabbage Patch company, Coleco, had made enough money to buy up the firm that made Scrabble and Parcheesi. Three years later, with the slump in sales, Coleco declared bankruptcy, and its primary assets – most notably those same Scrabble and Parcheesi games – were purchased by Hasbro.

The year of Cabbage Patch mania, 1984, also saw the birth of Masters of the Universe. Mattel's latest winner helped the company balance the success of the Barbie doll with a boys' toy. Masters of the Universe was a series of action figures that featured He-Man as the main character. In the first wave of sales fever, demand for He-Man eclipsed that for Barbie, generating $400 million in sales in 1985. But this He-Man fell as fast as he had risen, leaving Mattel with a big void in sales and warehouses full of unwanted figures.

Alongside the sentimental pleasures of dolls like the Cabbage Patch Kids and Sylvanian Family, a revolution was about to take place in children's hearts and minds ... We'd had ten years or more to get used to video games. It was well over a decade since Pong. But silicon-chip technology was growing exponentially, offering fantastic potential for games manufacturers ...

In 1983 the Japanese company Nintendo introduced its first Nintendo entertainment system to the United States. With an amazing fifty-two colours, realistic sound and high-speed action, the home-video games system eventually won over retailers who'd been initially sceptical: Atari had only recently gone bust, so why should this Japanese gadget have any more of a long-term future? The one thing you could say about dolls and soldiers was that children had been playing with them for centuries. But back in those simple days TV hadn't been around to drive the sales pitch home at every opportunity. And nowadays peers seemed to pressure like never before. Despite the early scepticism, the Nintendo entertainment system, along with games such as Super Mario Brothers and the Legend of Zelda, was destined to be the top-selling 'toy' of 1987 and

1988. Soon everyone was talking Donkey Kong and Crash Bandicoot; they were the Noddy and Sooty of the microchip generation.

Toy ideas seemed to be coming at us from around the globe. From the Eastern Bloc, from America and especially from the Far East. As well as its genius for electronics, Japan had a way with warrior toys of a slightly more traditional nature. In 1985, for instance, Transformers ruled the toy roost – chunky robots which could be changed into vehicles or weapons. Or were they cars which changed into robots?

Transformers had their origins back in 1974, when Japanese children's fascination for robots had inspired a range of toys known as Micromen. Like My Little Pony, these were no haphazard toys. Micromen had a detailed mythology behind them, tales that had been recounted for years in Japan's popular manga comic-books. The futuristic story was about an alien race of humanoids who had been floating through space for thousands of years before their capsules eventually crashed into the Earth's oceans. Water pollution mutated some of the new arrivals into the evil Acroyears, who plotted to conquer Earth. To defend their adopted home from domination, the good-guy Micromen designed giant mechanical robots to fight the Acroyears.

With this ready-made background story and a painstaking attention to colour and design details, the Micromen line was destined for huge success and continued for nearly ten years with all kinds of weird and wonderful variations on the basic theme: the Gun-Robo series, for instance, featured six robots, one of whom had a five-inch sword and a gun that could fire plastic pellets.

In the early 1980s, several American companies expressed interest in bringing similar 'transformer robots' to US children. Several of the original Micromen toys, made under licence and renamed Micronauts, had been released in America in the late seventies by the Mego Corporation, but US children found the concept strange and unfamiliar when compared to the normal trucks, cars and cowboy games they'd been used to. The product failed to take off, doomed by children's disinterest and a lack of targeted marketing.

However, others still believed in the idea. Hasbro knew the toys had potential and they realised what was missing from the marketing: the mythology. If the toys were marketed alongside the 'save the world' stories they would be a surefire hit. Working from old Micromen moulds, Hasbro created what came to be known as Transformers. As well as realistic trucks, cars and planes the line included mechanical animals and even household objects, including cassettes, a tape-player and guns. The toys had seemingly limitless potential. There were even Transformers with heads that were themselves Transformers, these 'Headmasters' supposedly coming from the year 2011. In a bizarre twist, one series, the Action Masters, were marketed as Transformers even though they didn't transform!

Whatever the cultural provenance, boys in the West loved them. The usual stories of Christmas season shortages were recycled in the media, with the now obligatory shocking tales of panicking parents being trampled in toyshop stampedes. Demand was huge and Hasbro's marketing was genius. For instance, several Transformers could be merged together to form giants known as Gestalts; so rather than children being happy with one of the toys, they had to buy three or four in order to create a single Gestalt.

In 1986, at the height of Transformer mania, came *Transformers: The Movie*. The film had a fabulous cast including *Star Trek*'s Leonard Nimoy and the legendary Orson Welles, co-starring with ex-*Monty Python* star Eric Idle. Set in the year 2005, the story centred on the Decepticons' conquest of Cybertron and the stationing of Autobots on Cybertron's moons and on Earth. As if that wasn't trouble enough, there was also Unicron, a planet that devoured other worlds. During the course of the movie many of the older characters were dramatically killed off, with new characters – and therefore potential new toy sales – stepping in to fill their places.

The toy firms knew that if they found a craze, they could cash in. By the mid-1980s children in the West had phenomenal spending power. Combine the weekly pocket-money allowances of Britain's children, for instance, and you could be looking at upwards of fifty million pounds' liquid capital. And that wasn't every year, but every week!

The company that benefited most from these little gold mines at the end of the decade was Nintendo. Christmas 1989 belonged to the Game Boy, a silicon-driven diversion which further blurred the line between children's toys and adults' amusements. The seventy-pound Game Boy was a battery-powered, hand-held video-game system that appealed to youngsters and yuppies alike. The graphics, by today's standards, were simple, but nations around the world were in thrall to the gadget.

But while all this video-game mania was going on, the good old yo-yo came back to establish itself as a hardy perennial, albeit ripe for a spot of updating. Enter the yo-yo with a brain, with free-spinning sleeve for longer 'sleeping' and a centrifugal spring-loaded clutch for automatic return when the rotation slowed to a certain rate. Soon after came transaxle yo-yos with ball-bearings that increased spin times immensely. It all went to prove that there's nothing like a bit of technology to add some spin.

But the toy trade was nothing if not a game of swings and roundabouts. In 1971 the Airfix company had expanded by acquiring the legendary Meccano from the bankrupted Line Brothers. With the legendary Dinky range of metal die-cast toys and Hornby-Dublo train sets now in its portfolio, Airfix assumed the title of Britain's leading toy manufacturer. But ten years later Airfix itself was broke. The kit range was still profitable, but the Meccano and Dinky sectors were in deep trouble and the company had to be bailed out by America's Palitoy. Kit production was moved to France and models began to appear with a 'Made in France' legend on the boxes.

In 1984 *Airfix Magazine* carried a feature in praise of the new kits being marketed by Humbrol. Previously known mostly for making the mini-tins of paint which most Airfix fans used on their finished kits, Humbrol had branched out. After acquiring a couple of European kit-makers, the firm reboxed the models and started to sell them under their own logo. No longer enjoying the luxury of having the market to itself and desperate to slim down, Airfix sold all of its railway and trackside ranges to Dapol. But even this last-ditch act couldn't save Airfix from a sticky situation and the continuing weaknesses made the company ripe for a takeover – by Humbrol.

1990s

As a parent, I can't help thinking that children today have less *fun* than we had. Their lives seem dominated by the race to acquire, to compete with a peer group that has no leader except some figure on TV, a figure who could be viewed as being equally manufactured and slickly marketed as the toys. Once the marketing machine cranks up around October, the kids don't stand a chance. Assaulted on all sides by TV ads, catalogues and their friends, they end up with their heads spinning faster than Linda Blair in *The Exorcist*. Choice has always been agonising, but now it is more so.

There's a wonderful irony in *Toy Story*. Its heroes are a bunch of traditional 1950s and 1960s toys who have been neglected in tear-jerking 'Puff the Magic Dragon' fashion. Mr Potato Head, a cowboy, a springy sausage dog, these are the toys that the new generation had turned its back on. But as heroes of a Hollywood blockbuster they became marketable commodities once again, with millions of kids clamouring for their own copies. Maybe that's what gave the film its appeal to adults – a warm glow brought on by the meting out of poetic justice. The double irony is that these lovable characters were all computer-generated, with not a loose thread, dodgy stuffing or peculiar odour about any of them. Antiseptic and digitally perfect, they nevertheless alerted kids to a lovability that they were missing out on.

TV's influence, too, comes in an equally sanitised package. The toy version of *Animal Hospital*, based on a BBC series, limits its services to cute puppies and kittens. No finger-nipping ferrets or fearsome iguanas here. None of the sets include a rubber glove or any suggestion of a rectal probe on a reluctant bovine. The puppy 'whimpers' and the kitten 'meows' (their quotes), but one gulp from the magic feeding bottle will make them better.

Steam engines aren't lovable, it seems, unless they have Thomas's grinning face on the smokebox door. If in doubt, stick a smiley face on it. The craze for spotting Eddie Stobart lorries has now filtered down to the shelves of Britain's toyshops. It is a sad reflection on society that the child strapped into his car seat like a trussed-up turkey has no better pastime than to spot this man's lorries, but we can't really blame Mr Stobart for that. However, having his lorries glorified isn't quite enough: Steady Eddie is now a fully fledged cartoon character and his lorry toys now come saddled with Steady Eddie's beaming fizzog. This tendency to cuteness in toys may be disturbing, but any parent would prefer it to another growing trend: obsessive collecting.

In America's gun culture, the fatal shooting of a warehouse guard in West Virginia in 1999 was nothing unusual. But the execution-style killing turned out to be the most sinister aspect of the worldwide Beanie Baby hysteria. Investigating police discovered that the slain security guard had a lucrative sideline in illicitly supplying the public with the hard-to-find toys. But he'd failed to pay for the last consignment of stolen Beanie Babies, hence the swift vengeance. The cutesy Beanie Babies had become dumb accessories to homicide.

Suddenly toys weren't so innocent. No longer fluffy play-things intended to make children smile — they now had other values. Toys had become a sinister currency: media stories created panic; parents got hysterical; demand transformed them into contraband. Passions reached fever pitch when the manu-facturers announced that production would cease for ever on the last day of 1999. Alerted to a new opportunity, organised gangs were busy robbing shops and warehouses. With collec-tors scrambling to snap up the remaining Beanies and rare edi-tions fetching hundreds of dollars, criminal activity was inevitable.

Most Beanie Baby collectors were harmless: children and old

ladies who cheered up every time they glanced at their babies sitting on the mantelpiece. At the loony end of the market there were nerdy guys who kept their Beanie Babies in glass cases, sealed against dust, never to feel a human touch. Just the kind of obsessives who hated gaps in their collection, so much so that they'd pay any price for a coveted item – and it wasn't hard to find criminals ready to rob and murder to meet the demand.

Cuddly and adorable with big goo-goo eyes, Beanie Babies like Pouch the Kangaroo, Spike the Rhinoceros and Claude the Crab wanted to be your special friend. They were the invention of Ty Warner, a fifty-five-year-old media-shy billionaire known as the Howard Hughes of the toy industry. As the sole owner of his company, the 250 million Beanie Babies sold in 1998 earned Warner the rather spooky title of 'Richest Toy-maker in the World' – estimated to be worth some seven billion dollars. The company's smart but forbidding office block in Chicago has no postal address other than a PO box. The phone number is ex-directory and trespassers are warned off. Staff were obliged to sign a secrecy pledge before joining the company, vowing never to discuss their boss or any aspect of the company's operations. Business associates were allowed to communicate only in writing. Since media sleuths could trace only two photographs of Ty Warner, there were doubts that he even existed.

Animals like Squealer the Pig and Pinchers the Lobster sold for around four pounds in the shops, but rare editions could fetch up to £1,250 on the black market. Collectors and criminals both gambled on the toys becoming prized. A massive second-hand trade grew up, fuelled by the Internet and prices spiralled. Billionaire Bear, created to celebrate one billion dollars' worth of Beanies sold, is now worth more than two thousand dollars itself. A Princess Bear, in memory of the late Princess of Wales, earned nearly seven million pounds for her memorial fund. When McDonald's gave away mini-Beanie Babies with their Happy Meals their supply – bought to last throughout the six-week promotion – was exhausted in three days. Clever marketeers increased the demand simply by restricting supplies. Beanie Babies were never advertised, nor sold in major toyshop chains such as Toys R Us. Since their debut in 1994, they were available only through small gift shops, and each design was 'retired' quickly, making older ones sought after.

In 1999 Warner stunned the toy industry by announcing that Beanie Babies were for the chop. No explanation was given. Speculation was rife. Why would Warner want to kill off a golden goose that had earned him billions and could yet earn him many times more? Spokesmen refused to elaborate, save to acknowledge that media reports of criminal activity had been a factor.

The final Beanie Baby, a small black bear, was known appropriately as The End.

No sooner had he departed the toyshops than the shelves were stacked with another money-spinner with seemingly limitless potential for profit. Pokémon was almost instantly denounced by US police as America's 'most dangerous hobby' – quite a claim from a country where sub-machine-guns are freely available for recreation. But as commercial hysteria and hard-nosed values filtered down from the adult world into schools and playgrounds, Pokémon cards were blamed for a wave of stabbings, beatings and robbings as kids strove to collect all the sets. If they couldn't get their cards fair and square they might as well take someone else's. 'It's become a war because such huge amounts of money are involved,' said an LA cop. 'Kids are literally fighting each other to get their hands on these cards.'

'This is far worse than the Cabbage Patch Doll craze,' said a policeman in Philadelphia after six children were arrested for attacks on classmates. 'There are Pokémon card sharps out there.' In California prosecutors filed charges against a thirteen-year-old boy from Orange County who was accused of stealing a classmate's Pokémon cards – and then running him over with his bicycle.

Bad publicity had dogged Pokémon from the start, even before it was exported to the West. In 1997 hundreds of Japanese children suffered seizures triggered by the flashing of the Pikachu character's lightning bolt on the Pokémon TV cartoons.

Pokémon – short for pocket monsters (and spookily pre-scient) – was the brainchild of Satoshi Tajiri, a Japanese games inventor who combined his childhood loves of monster movies and entomology. The game involves 155 creatures, each with its own special powers. The goal is to win as many of the colourful cards from opponents as possible.

While the appeal of Pokémon remained baffling to adults, a Nintendo spokesman gave his own interpretation: 'Pikachu and the other Pokémon characters look very cute, but if any-thing happens then they are ready to fight. Maybe that is why they appeal to Americans.'

But a simple card game is no longer enough to fill the corpo-rate coffers satisfactorily. The craze also spawned a Nintendo computer game, a cartoon TV series and a film which grossed thirty-five million pounds in its first five days (and was followed by two sequels). Throw in all the books, stuffed toys, key-rings, pencil cases, rubber balls and clothing and it adds up to worldwide sales of £3.8 billion.

With fighting rife in the playground many schools were moved to ban Pokémon cards and toys from the premises, which only confused parents who were using them as rewards for children getting good marks. 'It's difficult to know what to do,' said one dad. 'My daughter and her friends are totally caught up in this craze. I don't understand it at all and neither do any of the other parents I've spoken to.'

Packets of eleven Pokémon cards sold for about two pounds, but first-edition characters such as Charizard and Mew could fetch up to two hundred pounds in on-line auctions. Counter-feiting was rife and in 2000 US Customs officials seized fake cards worth fifteen million.

It's not raining men – it's raining Pokémon. Imagine, if you will, a shower of Pokémon cards. In the kitchen. Little mon-sters fluttering to earth where they will, into the bin, into the washing-up bowl, on to the gas cooker. No, it isn't a freak meteorological event, for these are Pokémon cards, dozens and dozens of them – fifty quid's worth in fact.

The child who owned them had written to his grandma to tell her he'd been offered a place on the school trip to France, but couldn't go because his parents couldn't afford the £70 necessary for the deposit. Dear old gran duly indulged her distant grandson by sending an envelope with four crisp banknotes inside a sellotaped envelope. Kid has struck lucky here! Slipping past his unwitting parents, the boy heads straight into town to blow the lot on Pokémon cards and a mini BMX bike (another parallel craze).

But such crimes rarely go undiscovered. Dads are too smart and children make careless criminals. They never plan their alibis carefully enough. So when dad finds out he hits the roof – as do the shiny brand new Pokémon cards, all of them, flickering and shining in the spring sunshine they fall to the lino. Infuriated by the ridiculous monsters' faces as much as the crime itself, Dad consumes a whole bottle of Muscadet. Kid vanishes. Dad, to avoid nasty domestic accidents (71 per cent of home fatalities are due to slipping on something) picks them all up and reassembles the stack into something approaching pristine condition. Despite a twinge of sympathy for the collection mania (didn't he collect bubblegum stickers and tea cards?) he hides them away in a corner, never to be seen again. By the time he feels like restoring them to his child the Pokémon craze will have passed and the only ones to profit from the incident will be some savvy entrepreneurs in downtown Tokyo.

Such incidents prove that the world is changing, but in some ways things are as they always were. Take Christmas. Sharing carpet space with the kid twiddling the buttons on Grand Theft Auto is another kid who stares in horror at the 1,000 pieces of a Chad Valley 'cute kitten in a basket' jigsaw puzzle. It's a team effort: Grandma sifts patiently through the pieces, finding first the four corners and then all the straight edges; slowly, to the background screams of murder and mayhem on the pixelated streets of an American crime hell, the pastoral exercise in kitty care begins to take shape. People are basically having much the same Christmas as they always did. I can imagine, back in 1966, Gran grumbling about changing values when the same puzzle was being assembled alongside the fantasy screechings of her grandson lying prone on the carpet playing with a Corgi James Bond car.

But Gran was right all along – it's the jigsaw puzzle that's still here. Walk into Woolworth's and there they are – of pussycats and country cottages and steam trains. Tradition sells. Strangely enough, no one wants a jigsaw of a mountain bike or Millennium Dome or Canary Wharf. We're talking about enduring values. A jigsaw puzzle, by default almost, has to be of something ultra-traditional, as befits its status as an old-time activity. Puzz3D added (literally) an extra dimension to the jigsaw-puzzle world – and a gigantic price tag to boot. But it wasn't space-age stuff we wanted but the comforting landmarks of Big Ben, Tower Bridge and the Orient Express.

We use toys as an indicator of changing values, and in many ways they are. At the same time they provide proof of how little values really change. Despite all the silliest hype, it's silly to believe that human nature can be changed by marketing. Style and form may change, but the content is essentially the same. WCW wrestling figures are just the toy soldiers of 1900 moved on a century – except that now they boast Realscan technology, whatever that might be. Essentially the toy is still powered by a child's nimble fingers, a bit of aggro and a lot of imagination. Action Man is now as likely to be found on a BMX bike or roller-blades as in a Jeep, but the way in which he is perilously manoeuvred into situations of extreme danger remains the same. Toy cars may now be Mitsubishis rather than Aston Martins, but they're still pushed along by kids who want to grow up and drive for real. Anakin Skywalker is simply the new Dan Dare.

Dolls are still here by the dozen, dressed in 2001's styles, of course, but basically with no more personality or reality than that which is invested in them by the child. No toy ever really comes into significance until it enters a child's imagination. Families still sit in the wreckage of wrapping paper and

Christmas dinner playing whodunnits, howdoits and howthe-helldyaplayits? Kiddies still impatiently explain the rules of games to their grans and grandads, just as Victorian kids no doubt were infuriated by their elders' failure to grasp the rules of Lotto. Monopoly, Cluedo, Scrabble, Connect4 and Frustration all still sell by the truckload. There's also the bizarre but perennial favourite Operation, in which gleeful kids remove various bones and organs from a plastic body: 'Operate Now!' invites the box lid. Mousetrap, one of the true classics, is still going strong after thirty-odd years. Gimmick versions of these games made brief appearances for double the price, but quickly vanished. Scrabbling for batteries to play Monopoly – whatever next?

In December 2000 our local Woolworth's was stacked to the ceiling with buckets of Lego. Yes, buckets – not well-mannered boxes any more. Like KFC chicken bits, everything these days comes in a greed-satisfying bucket. But what's inside is the same as it was forty years ago, give or take an electronic gizmo or two.

Meccano is still around a century later, and probably will be in the year 2101. Toy soldiers, probably one of the oldest play-things of all, still seem to be going strong. But these are more politically correct days. Pretending to be a smart Tommy slicing up a few crazed Zulus may have been fine a century ago, but such pretend games have become less acceptable. A new range of 'historically accurate' action figures, part of the 21st Century Toy Company's Ultimate Soldier series, caused considerable consternation when they went on sale. They weren't just good ol' GIs with a pack of gum to spare and a winning way with kiddies: the range included Germans. Though still regarded by many as the bad guys in both World Wars, the manufacturers would not be dissuaded from using the purplest of war-glorying prose on the packaging. No miserable cowardly Huns, these were German paratroopers with 'supreme soldierly skills' or Panzer Grenadiers who 'struck fear into the heart of the world', and mini-versions of the Wehrmacht infantry whose deeds would still seem all too real to the old folk who remember the occupied Russia of 1941. After complaints, the twelve-inch German figures, which cost a whopping thirty dollars each, disappeared from some toyshops. When queried about their disappearance the staff of one Long Island shop told irate customers that they'd sold out and were not expecting any more.

The toy-makers have to tread much more carefully these days. The Walt Disney Corporation was forced to change a sombrero-wearing character in the *Toy Story 2* video game because the mustachioed villain, complete with bullet bandolier angered many Hispanics who complained that it was a damaging stereotype. Worse than that, this stereotype was doomed to die, since anyone playing the game had to kill the 'Mexican' villain in order to advance to the next level. 'Degrading, dehumanising, stereotyping Mexicans as villains,' said one of the protesters (manifestly not wearing a sombrero or pistol) picketing the California HQ of the company. 'It's a virtual game of genocide, the way we see it, because they're being ethno-specific.' Anxious not to offend Disney cranked up the saccharine diplomacy, expressing great regret that any portion of their game caused offence. 'There was a mistake made in its creation,' said a spokeswoman (who sounded as if she was apologising on behalf of God for his dysfunctional Eden figures). 'We plan to change the character.'

Talking of stereotypes, Barbie is still with us. She's over forty years old, but remains stuck in a weird undefinable age group. With legs like contoured matchsticks and an anatomically impossible figure, Barbie is a role-model like no other although she still can't make up her mind *which* role: show-jumper, hippy chick, *Baywatch* babe or caring childminder? Well, why can't a girl be all of them?

In 1955 Barbie gained a little sibling, Baby Sister Kelly, and in 1997 a disabled friend in a wheelchair, Share a Smile Becky. Baby Sister Chrissy was added to the Barbie family in 1999, the year when Barbie herself hit forty. The celebrations recognised special women of achievement (Ambassadors of Dreams), including: (predictably) Ruth Handler, the woman who

A 1990's childhood (Corbis)

created the first Barbie doll; Muriel Siebert, the first woman on the New York Stock Exchange; Rosie O'Donnell, an award-winning talk-show host; Anne Moore, president of *People* magazine; Dr Sylvia Earle, a renowned marine biologist; and Jackie Joyner–Kersee, one of the greatest female athletes in the world.

Approximately one billion Barbie dolls have been sold over her four decades, making her the bestselling fashion doll in almost every major global market, with worldwide annual sales of one and a half billion dollars.

Strangely enough, Barbie doesn't have a little sister who is a child labourer...

In the past few years attention has focused on the poor record in health and safety and workers' rights in the toy industry. The worst incident was in 1993 when a fire broke out at a toy factory in Thailand. One hundred and eighty-eight workers were killed – the majority of them young women and girls, some as young as thirteen. They had been locked in the factory to prevent theft. There were no fire alarms and stairways were obstructed by flammable materials. Once alight, the materials gave off poisonous fumes. Many who survived the fire and fumes did so because they jumped from windows, their falls cushioned by the dead bodies of their workmates below.

It was not an isolated incident. Fires are common in Asian sweatshops. Workers are paid very low wages for long hours without rest or toilet breaks. Those who try to improve conditions are fired or worse. The toy industry is supplied from thousands of small factories set up to avoid inspections, keep wages low and union and human rights activists out. The factories subcontract to all the biggest names in the toy manufacturing world.

In spite of activists' efforts the child labour continues and toyshops show no signs of making a stand against it. They, it seems, have more important things to worry about – like the corruption of Western children. Woolworth's and Hamleys both refused to stock the controversial nine-inch-high Eminem doll created by a New York company, which seems like an odd sort of morality considering the toys that they *do* sell. The doll was a pretty good likeness, sporting tattoos, wearing a mask and wielding a chainsaw. Psychologists warned parents that buying the doll would be a seal of approval to Eminem's attitudes. Another psychologist expressed alarm that children as young as eleven were naming Eminem as their favourite performer.

Having a doll modelled on yourself was the ultimate sign of having arrived! Eminem would get a royalty of about two pounds on each doll sold, but Woolworth's were not prepared to contribute to his bank balance, saying the doll did not fit with their family image. Hamleys admitted that the Britney Spears and Hear'Say dolls were lucrative but explained its decision with the understated, 'Eminem is a bit naughtier.'

It was left to untraditional sources to sell the dolls: Tower Records claimed they were 'pretty cool'.

As has always been the way with teen culture, Eminem's

appeal is a mystery to his fans' parents. In much the same way, kids and their parents don't see eye to eye where other toys are concerned, but recently a strange reversal has occurred.

While the ten-year-olds seem content to chatter on their mobiles, their parents – dads anyway – are thronging the model shops and toy fairs in hot pursuit of old Airfix kits and Dinky toys from the sixties. Now well off, they can indulge themselves and buy the toys they were never able to afford as youngsters. They queue up to pay fifty pounds for a car which would have cost them two shillings in 1962 and which they would have treated with clumsy indifference. Now such cars are centrepieces, lovingly displayed on shelves and in cabinets.

But wait – what do we really mean by the catch-all phrase 'collectors' item'? Is it not in all honesty a euphemism for something a lot more complex? 'Collectors' item' imbues the object with a *faux*-serious quality, but let's not be so pretentious: all these guys flocking to the toy fair are not lower-end antique collectors; they're just blokes who want to be kids again and, by golly, how they miss their childhoods. The joys of adulthood, are nowhere near as satisfying as holding a Corgi Chipperfields' lorry or a plastic, battery-operated Dalek. For the Dalek, if it could speak, would not just say, 'Exterminate!' ad nauseam, it would whisper, 'Hey, kid, remember me and you, 1966, in your back garden ...' The Dalek is our new spirit of remembrance.

But why is the toy fair so overwhelmingly male, as blokey as a railway open day or a computer club? Maybe it's because women are always in touch with themselves – and men aren't until it's far too late. That's why they haunt such places, looking for those links with a time when they were untroubled by whiskers and hormones and a need to compete against young men who know much more about double-glazing. You can almost hear them praying: 'Find me that garden again, Lord, when it was just me and the Dinky toys and the occasional wriggly worm, when tea was on the table and Mum's hair was still as red as a forest fire.'

Call me a silly sentimentalist, but it makes me wonder,

what's happened to Britain's toyshops? This little town of ours had several, all stocked with boxes from floor to ceiling. You could pick up toys at the newsagent's, in the post office, even the local old-fashioned grocer always had the album for sticking in the Brooke Bond tea cards. What choice is there now for the children? It's between Toys R Us (a ten-mile drive away, stuck on some arterial road) and the Argos catalogue. There'll be no little noses pressed up against the windows of these corporate enterprises. An evening walk will inspire no dreams, get no little feet stamping in anticipation or frustration. Toys are no longer bought with shillings from Mum's purse; in the hi-tech warehouse dolls go to their new owners at the swipe of a credit card and the signing of a sales voucher.

At least toy buying is so much easier for twenty-first-century parents. However did all those old-fashioned mums and dads manage without the snippets of 'Customer Information' provided by thoughtful retailers such as Argos: 'Always choose toys that suit both the age and ability of your child.' So helpful! Such insight! How would anyone have remembered otherwise? Without such reminding, dumb parents might have chosen Meccano for their toddler or Teletubby figures for their teenager! But who decides? Does Argos have a child psychologist paid a handsome retainer to pass a verdict on each toy?

Memories are best when they have an element of stubborn subjectivity: exaggeration always makes a better story. But it was predictable that the toy trade would cash in on nostalgia by sponsoring a competition to find the Toy of the Century. 'I've seldom seen men and women so excited,' said an industry boss commenting on the hysteria. Such a contest was never going to be more than an all too predictable publicity stunt, with the aim being to grab newspaper inches – a ploy with which journalists willingly complied. Postmodern hacks gleefully filled the pages of the broadsheets with semi-serious, semi-ironic features on Barbie, Dinky and even Ker-Plunk. Nevertheless, with votes logged by the public via the Internet, the results are interesting.

Favourites were Lego and the Teddy bear; others on the

shortlist were Barbie and Action Man. There was more fuss over what had been missed out and people seemed to take the omissions personally. Radio phone-ins and newspaper letter pages were buzzing with indignant thirty- and forty-somethings. Not even to nominate Meccano, Hornby train sets and Dinky and Corgi was tantamount to saying those who'd played with them had wasted their childhoods on also-rans. Also absent was the Spirograph and Nintendo Game Boy.

Nominations for 'Game of the Century' were also causes for contention. Most of the obvious candidates — Scrabble, Monopoly and Trivial Pursuit — were included but where were Cluedo and Pictionary? Men with beards took particular exception to the omission of Dungeons and Dragons.

Crazes of the Century was probably the most interesting category. The top ones were the hula hoop, supposedly dating from ancient Egypt — are there any hieroglyphics to prove it? Was one buried in Tutankhamun's tomb? — but not a toy craze until the late 1950s. Similarly with the yo-yo, supposedly a favourite toy of the ancient Greeks, but I don't see one on the Elgin Marbles. Crazes that failed to be nominated included Clackers from 1971 and POGS, the bottle-top game that swept the world in 1995. Frisbees, which were originally the tin lids off pies made by the Frisbee Pie Company, didn't make it on to the shortlist — probably because they hardly count as a craze, being still as popular on the beach and in the park as they were originally. Also missing, amazingly, was the Rubik's Cube.

Considering the potential electorate, the actual votes cast seem rather thin on the ground. Toy of the Century turned out to be Lego — probably a justified choice considering its versatility. By the middle of 2001 though it had polled only a measly 588 votes. Monopoly had rather more fans, it seemed, easily winning Game of the Century category with 755 votes. The Craze of the Century was the yo-yo. Compared with the transitory nature of many fads — Clackers, Space Hoppers, POGS, etc. — the yo-yo is a hardy perennial, an established childhood accessory rather than a true craze.

Subbuteo fans became very nervous in the mid-1990s when

makers Waddington's were bought out by American giants Hasbro. Although the basic Subbuteo sets were still made, the large range of accessories and teams were quickly trimmed. For a time, Premier League sponsorship seemed to be the most profitable option and the Premiership teams, with logos and badges, were some of the best sets ever produced. The Subbuteo name was even used to market a set of football cards. But shortly after Subbuteo's fiftieth anniversary rumours began that Hasbro were intending to axe production altogether in January 2000. The announcement made big news and featured on all the major TV channels. Whether the whole thing was orchestrated is debatable (it wouldn't have been the first time that companies had tried emotional blackmail to revive flagging sales) but Hasbro were so overwhelmed by the outcry that Subbuteo was granted a stay of execution. The 2000 Toys R Us catalogue featured three boxed Subbuteo sets: Premiership, Man United and a de-luxe version. There were rumours that more Premiership teams would soon be available. Good news for die-hard fans but most people were forced to concede that the detail and atmosphere of the latest computer football games made Subbuteo look sadly old hat.

A similar situation occurred with Cluedo. When it was announced that the Reverend Green was to 'retire' there was an outcry. The manufacturers not only upset dedicated Cluedo fans past and present, but also the clergy, who inferred that vicars were being labelled old hat and irrelevant in our trendy society. So the campaign to reinstate the redundant Reverend proceeded on two fronts, thereby assuring maximum interest and sales of Cluedo. He was eventually reprieved, but who's to say that the makers of Cluedo ever really intended to bump him off?

Maybe Cluedo's makers were orchestrating a cynical marketing campaign. Maybe they just realised that some things should remain the same. The old toys are all alive and well: you can still buy a toy fire engine with an extendable ladder, a police car, a tractor towing a milk tanker behind it. There are lorries and garages and helicopters. Most of them would have been around fifty years ago; some of them were around a century ago. Computer games have one vital element missing: there's nothing to touch. So much of toys is to do with the senses: touch, taste and smell, just as much as sight and sound. The computer game is locked away in hermetically sealed non-reality. Exciting, yes, but ultimately non-engaging.

Could this be why mobile phones are now so prized? They feel satisfyingly heavy in the hand; they have a factory-fresh plasticky fragrance; they make funny noises; and they twinkle. By all the criteria, mobiles are an excellent toy. It's just a shame that children have to hock themselves indefinitely. It may be a toy, but unless you keep paying the life goes out of it! Unless you buy your top-up cards its lights go out, its noises stop and it turns into a dead weight in your hand.

Our collective vision of the nursery – see a score of period dramas – usually includes a rocking-horse, a Teddy bear and a few Dinky cars: childhood reduced to a kind of shorthand. Why, we haven't even progressed past the sixties; we don't want to face it. Clackers and Chopper Bikes and Connect4 don't belong in our fondly remembered past. None has yet achieved holy status. Recent TV programmes about the 1970s only look at them with a kind of squeamish embarrassment; they are still things we ridicule.

Perhaps it is time to remix our vision of childhood and see it as a world of toys including Teddies next to Sony Playstations, dolls sitting alongside Pokémon cards and train sets competing for affection with mobile phones. Perhaps that is what the children of today will see through their rose-tinted glasses in 2050.

INDEX

Italic page numbers refer to illustrations.

accidents *see* safety
action figures 141–2, 170
Action Man 142, 181
Adolph, Peter 89
advertising 130
aeroplanes 3, 18, 72, 87–8
Airfix 91, 101–2, 173–4
airships 72
Aquinas, Thomas 32
arcade games 155–7, 170
arctophilia 16
Atari 155–7, 170

bagatelle 70
balls, rubber 59–60
Barbie 129–30, 154, 183–4
Bassett-Lowke, Wenman J 14–15
battleships 67, 86
Bayko construction sets 135–8
Beanie Babies 176–8
bicycles *see* cycles
Blake, William 26
BMX 162, 180, 181
board games 64, 120, 142
  chess 4, 38
  Cluedo 111–12, 189

draughts 38
Edwardian 18–19
Game of the Century 188
Ludo 111–12
Monopoly 79–83, 88, 188
Mousetrap 3, 135, 182
political 20–2
Scrabble 3, 95, 110–11
Snakes and Ladders 19
television-based 154–5
Victorian 19
boats 3
boomerangs 63
Bradley, Milton 30
Britain, William 11
British Marbles Board of Control 27
Brunot, James 110–11
Bushnell, Nolan 156
Butts, Alfred 110–11

Cabbage Patch Kids 16, 33, 168–70
cap guns 21, 57, 104, 130
cards 24–5
  collections 145–7, 153
  fortune-telling 64
  playing cards 47, 62, 87
  POGS 24

Pokémon 146, 178–80
  trading 146–7
Carroll, Lewis 110
cars
  Corgi 4, 131–3
  dancing 71
  die-cast 131–5
  Dinky 2, 4, 77, 107, 133–4
  Hot Wheels 135, 160–1
  Matchbox 2, 92–4, 160–1
  pedal 36, 41–4
  radio-controlled 1
  Tonka 107
  Transformers 171–2
carts 42
  see also trolleys
cereal box gifts 146–7
Chapman, Percy 61–2
Chasse, Paul 138–9
chemistry sets 3, 56, 77, 144
chess 4, 38
Christiansen, Ole Kirk 92
Christmas 1–4, 118–20, 152,
    180–2
  panic buying 169, 172
cinema 109
  merchandise 63, 68, 132–3, 175
  toy-based 96, 172, 175
clockwork toys 53–4, 71, 94–5,
    110
  see also mechanisation
Cluedo 111–12, 189
collections 2, 5, 186
  Beanie Babies 176–8
  cards 145–7, 153
  Pokémon 146, 178–80
  soft toys 166–7
  Teddy bears 16

comics 116
construction sets 9–10, 52–4,
    135–8
  see also Lego; Meccano
Corbett, Harry 96, 116
Corbett, Matthew 116
Corgi toys 4
  see also cars
Cowboys and Indians 68–70, 103,
    147–8
Cowen, Lionel 13–15
crazes
  Craze of the Century 188
  hula hoops 5, 115, 188
  marketing 172–3
  pogo sticks 40, 41, 114
  Pokémon 178–80
  Rubik's Cube 163–6
  skateboards 161–2, 188
  yo-yos 78–9, 115, 173, 188
cycles 36, 41–3, 121–2, 162

Darrow, Charles 79–83
diabolos 33–4, 78
dice games 64
  see also board games
die-casting 92–3, 131–5
Dinky toys 2, 4, 77, 107, 133–4
  see also cars
Dismal Desmond 61–2
Disney 33, 68, 70, 183
dolls 3, 4, 51–2, 113
  Barbie 129–30, 154, 183–4
  boys 124–6, 141–2
  ceramic 50–1
  German 49
  innovations 32, 48, 112,

115–16, 142
Italian 48, 112
prams 107–8
propaganda 33
racial stereotypes 32–3, 48, 50,
    73–4
role-playing 45
Royalty 72–3
safety 23, 113
sexism 98–9
Sindy 131, 154
dominoes 4, 38
draughts 38
Duncan, Donald 78–9

electricity sets 77
Eminem 185–6
endorsement 96–7, 108–9, 118,
    129, 131
Etch-A-Sketch 138–9
Evripoze system 68

fatal incidents *see* safety
films *see* cinema
Find Alf Smith 19–20
fireworks 57–8
fortune-telling 64
Freemans of Birmingham 51
fulking (marbles) 25–9
Furbies 33

Game Boys 4, 173
Game of the Century 188
gameplay 27–8, 30

German tinplate 11
GI Joe 141–2
Gilbert, A. C. 9–10
guns
    air 57
    cap 21, 57, 104, 130
    Cowboys and Indians 68–9
    merchandise 102–3
    pop 22–3
    safety 22, 69
    spud 104
    water pistols 22, 104
Guyer, Reyn 128

Handler, Ruth 183
Hanetsuki 25
Hassall, John 35
hobby horses 41–2
Hoffman, Abbie 79
Hop Rods 127–8
Hornby, Frank 7–8, 77
Hot Wheels 135, 160–1
hula hoops 5, 115, 188
human rights 184–5

in-line skates 36
indoor sports games 64–5, 65,
    70–1, 158–60
    see also Subbuteo

Japan, traditional toys 24–5
jigsaw puzzles 23–4, 38, 64–5, 84,
    139, 180–1
Johnson, Amy 72

Ker-Plunk 187
kites 18, 24–5, 59
Kitmaster 91–2
kits *see* scale models
Kove, Nicholas 101
Krazy Zoo 74

Laczi, Tibor 164–5
Lego 1, 2, 92, 182
    market domination 137–8
    Space Kits 158
    Toy of the Century 187–8
Lerner, George 96
Lloyd, Harold 63
Loch Ness Monster 83
Ludo 111–12

McVicker, Joe 113
Magie, Lizzie 79, 83
magnetic toys 11, 115–16
Magnusson, Magnus 154
Mamod Steam Engine 149–50
manga 171
marbles 25–9
mascots 61, 72, 109
Mastermind 154–5
Matchbox toys 92–4
    see also cars
Meccano 3, 7–9, 52–3, 182
    competitions 91
    innovations 74–5, 77
    mechanisation 8, 52, 91, 138
    plastic 137
    wartime shortage 86–7
Meccano Magazine 8–9, 75, 91
mechanisation

Dinky toys 77
German tinplate 11
Hornby clockwork trains 53–4
Meccano 8, 52, 91, 138
stuffed toys 60–2
menko 24
merchandise 3, 5
    cinema 63, 68, 132–3, 175
    comics 116
    1953 Coronation 95
    Disney 33, 68
    guns 102–3
    jigsaw puzzles 139
    Loch Ness Monster 83
    Pokémon 179
    pop music 139, 185–6
    Star Wars 157–8, 164
    television 118, 131, 133–5, 140,
        175–6
Merlin, John 35
meteorology sets 143
Micromen 171–2
microscopes 144–5
miniature BMX 180, 181
mobile phones 1, 3, 4, 152, 186,
    190
model aeroplanes *see* aeroplanes
model boats *see* boats
model railways *see* railway sets
Moksha-Patamu 19
Monopoly 79–83, 88, 188
Mousetrap 3, 135, 182
Mr Potato Head 96–7, 175
Museum of Childhood,
    Edinburgh 30
musical toys 3, 58–9, 130
My Little Pony 5, 16, 166

National Doll and Glass Eye
  Manufacturing Co 51
Negro Mother Association 32
Nintendo 157, 170–1
Noise Abatement Society 140

Old Daddy Tin Whiskers 11
Operation 182
Orwell, George 169

painting sets 56
Pankhurst, Emily 24
Parents for Responsibilty in the
  Toy Industry 141
Parker Brothers 81–3, 84–5
patents 10, 13, 17, 36, 68
patriotism 20–2
pedal cars 36, 41–4
pinball machines 70
pirates 105
plastic figures 101
Plasticine 58
Play-Doh 113–14
playing cards see cards
Playstations 1, 3, 4, 157
playsuits 63, 68–70, 103
Plimpton, James 36
pogo sticks 40, *41*, 114, 127
POGS 24
Pokémon 146, 178–80
politics 20–2, 23–4, 73
Pong 155–7, 170
pop guns 22–3
pop music 139, 185–6
Pot Shot snooker 34
practical jokes 37–8, 97

Pratt, Anthony 111
product placement 33, 55, 107
  see also merchandise
propaganda 17, 18, 21–2, 24,
  45–9
  dolls 33
  Hitler masks 86
  war games 87
puppets
  celebrity 96, 116–18
  racial stereotypes 98
  ventriloquist 113

racial stereotypes 182–3
  dolls 32–3, 48, 50, 73–4
  puppets 98
radio 62–3
radio-controlled cars 1
'rag and bone' men 65
rag books 34–5
Rag Flock Act 1951 113
railway sets 5, 11–15
  Airfix 91
  Bing 55
  electric 55–6, 75–7
  gauges 11–12, 76
  Hornby 5, 53–6, 75, 91
  Hornby-Dublo 150–2
  Kitmaster 91–2
  Lionel 14
  Marklin 12
Ring Taw 27–8
  see also marbles
Roberts, Xavier 'Happy' 168
robots 171–2
rocking-horses 43–4, 109
role-playing 45, 86, 106–7, 107–8

roller-skates 35–6, 124
Roosevelt, Theodore 17
rubber 59–60, 97
Rubik, Erno 163–6
Rubik's Cube 163–6, 188

safety
  balloons 60
  Beanie Babies 176–8
  dolls 23, 113
  guns 22, 69
  Hop Rods 127
  manufacture 184–5
  materials 64
  pedal cars 44
  railway sets 15
  skateboards 161–2
  soft toys 167–8
  toy appliances 107
St Dunstan's charity 67
Saugman, Dr Axel 75
scale models 67, 86, 87–8, 91–4, 102
Scalextric 95
sci-fi 99, 102–3, 105, *117*, 157, 171–2
scooters 1, *35*, 36–7, 41–3, 121–3
Scrabble 3, 95, 110–11
seaside toys 49–50
sexism, dolls 98–9
shove ha'penny 70, 71
Sindy 131, 154
singing games 31
skateboards 161–2, 188
skipping 31, 43, 58
Slinkys 97

Snakes and Ladders, Hindu origins 19
soldiers 2, 3, 63, 86
  contemporary 182–3
  plastic 101
  tin 23
solitaire 4
Space Invaders 155
spinning tops 59
Spirograph 188
Spitzmesser, Gordon 127
sponsorship 188–9
  see also merchandise; product placement
spud guns 104
squails (tiddlywinks) 29–31, 71
Stadden, Charles 158
stamp-collecting 87
Star Wars 157–8, 164
steam engines 149–50
stuffed toys 33, 60–2, 74
  see also dolls, Teddy bears
  Beanie Babies 176–8
  Cabbage Patch Kids 168–70
  collections 66–7
  Sylvanian Family 167
stunting kites 59
Subbuteo 89–91, 158–60, 188–9
sweatshops 184–5
Sylvanian Family 167

Tajiri, Satoshi 179
Tamagotchi 16
t'an ch'i 29–30
Teddy bears 1–4, 15–18, 32, 105–6
television 62, 130

board games 154–5
celebrity puppets 96, 116–18
merchandise 118, 131, 133–5,
  140, 175–6
Thunderbirds 134
tiddlywinks 29–31, 71
tin soldiers 23
Tinker Toys 10
Tonka toys 107
torches 120
Toy of the Century 187–8
Toy Story 96, 175
toyshops 1–3
Trade Board (Toy Manufacturing)
  Order 1926 66
trademarks 78–9, 94, 111
Trades Description Act 62
trading cards 146–7
train sets *see* railway sets
Transformers 171–2
Tri-ang News magazine 108–9
tricycles *see* cycles
Trivial Pursuit 155
trolleys 123
Twiddlers 64
Twister 128–9

Upton, Florence 73

ventriloquism 113
Victorian board games 19
video games 155–7, 190
  Atari 155–7, 170
  Game Boy 4, 173
  Nintendo 157, 170–1
  Playstation 1, 3, 4, 157
  Pokémon 179
  racial stereotypes 183
Viewmasters 148, *149*

war games 87
war toys 23, 46–7, 100, 141–2
war-kites 18
Warner, Ty 177
water pistols 22, 104
Who Wants to Be a Millionaire
  155
Women's International League for
  Peace and Freedom 141
Wright, John Lloyd 10
Wrigley, William Jr 113
writing sets 56

yakkodako kites 25
yo-yos 78–9, 115, 173, 188

Zeppelins 11, 18